This book belongs to

_____

...a woman after God's own heart.

Pursuing Godliness

Elizabeth George

HARVEST HOUSE PUBLISHERS
Eugene, Oregon 97402

Cover by Terry Dugan Design, Minneapolis, Minnesota

Acknowledgments

As always, thank you to my dear husband, Jim George, M.Div., Th.M., for your able assistance, guidance, suggestions, and loving encouragement on this project.

Contents

Foreword

Before You Begin

1. Encouraging Words...9
1 TIMOTHY 1:1-2

2. Watching Out for False Teachers...15
1 TIMOTHY 1:3-11

3. Giving Thanks for God's Mercy...22
1 TIMOTHY 1:12-17

4. Exhorting Young Timothy...27
1 TIMOTHY 1:18-20

5. Praying God's Way...33
1 TIMOTHY 2:1-8

6. Learning About Your Role...39
1 TIMOTHY 2:9-15

7. Instructing Church Leaders...47
1 TIMOTHY 3:1-7

8. Obtaining God's Reward...52
1 TIMOTHY 3:8-13

9. Ministering Faithfully...58
1 TIMOTHY 3:11

10. Pursuing Godliness...64
1 TIMOTHY 3:14-16

11. Identifying False Teachers...70
1 TIMOTHY 4:1-5

12. Exercising Yourself in Godliness...75
1 TIMOTHY 4:6-16

13. Caring for Others...80
1 TIMOTHY 5:1-2

14. Caring for Widows...85
1 TIMOTHY 5:3-8

15. Giving to Others...90
1 TIMOTHY 5:9-10

16. Living Above Reproach...95
1 TIMOTHY 5:11-16

17. Honoring Leaders...100
1 TIMOTHY 5:17-18

18. Examining Leaders...105
1 TIMOTHY 5:19-25

19. Serving in the Workplace...110
1 TIMOTHY 6:1-2

20. Recognizing False Teachers...115
1 TIMOTHY 6:3-5

21. Loving Money...121
1 TIMOTHY 6:6-10

22. Fighting the Good Fight of Faith...127
1 TIMOTHY 6:11-16

23. Handling Riches...133
1 TIMOTHY 6:17-19

24. Guarding the Treasure...139
1 TIMOTHY 6:20-21

25. A Final Word...144
SUMMARY OF 1 TIMOTHY

How to Study the Bible...147
Notes...153
Bibliography...155

Foreword

For some time I have been looking for Bible studies that I could use each day that would increase my knowledge of God's Word. In my search, I found myself struggling between two extremes: Bible studies that required little time but also had little substance, or studies that were in-depth and demanded more time than I could give. I discovered that I wasn't alone—there were many other women like me who were busy yet desired to spend quality time studying God's Word.

That's why I became excited when Elizabeth George shared her desire to create a series of women's Bible studies that offered in-depth lessons that could be completed in just 15-20 minutes per day. When she completed the first study—on Philippians—I was eager to try it out. I had already studied Philippians many times, but this was the first time I had come to understand exactly how the whole book fit together and how it can truly be lived out in my life. Each lesson was simple but insightful—and was written especially to apply to me as a woman!

In the Woman After God's Own Heart™ Bible study series, Elizabeth takes you step by step through the Scriptures, sharing wisdom she has gleaned from more than 20 years as a women's Bible teacher. The lessons are rich and meaningful because they're rooted in God's Word and have been lived out in Elizabeth's life. Her thoughtful and personable guidance makes you feel as though you are studying right alongside her—as if she is personally mentoring you in the greatest aspiration you could ever pursue: to become a woman after God's own heart.

If you're looking for Bible studies that can help you grow stronger in your knowledge of God's Word even in the most demanding of schedules, I know you'll find this series to be a welcome companion in your daily walk with God.

—LaRae Weikert
Editorial Managing Director,
Harvest House Publishers

Before You Begin

*I*n my book *A Woman After God's Own Heart*™, I describe such a woman as one who ensures that God is first in her heart and the Ultimate Priority of her life. Then I share that one crucial way this desire can become reality is by nurturing a heart that abides in God's Word. To do so means that you and I must develop a root system anchored deep in God's Word.

Before you launch into this Bible study, take a moment to think about these aspects of a root system produced by the regular, faithful study of God's Word:

- *Roots are unseen*—You'll want to set aside time in solitude—"underground" if you will—to immerse yourself in God's Word and grow in Him.

- *Roots are for taking in*—Alone and with your Bible in hand, you'll want to take in and feed upon the truths of the Word of God and ensure your spiritual growth.

- *Roots are for storage*—As you form the habit of looking into God's Word, you'll find a vast, deep reservoir of divine hope and strength forming for the rough times.

- *Roots are for support*—Do you want to stand strong in the Lord? To stand firm against the pressures of life? The routine care of your roots through exposure to God's Word will cultivate you into a remarkable woman of endurance.[1]

I'm glad you've chosen this study out of my A Woman After God's Own Heart™ Bible study series. My prayer for you is that the truths you find in God's Word through this study will further transform your life into the image of His dear Son and empower you to be the woman you seek to be: a woman after God's own heart.

In His love,

Elizabeth George

Lesson 1

Encouraging Words

*I*magine moving far away from family and friends. You're in a new church environment. The church is well established, but not without its problems. Plus you've been asked to give leadership to that church, not by the people in the church, but by someone from the outside. Thankfully, you and I will not likely have to worry about this type of scenario!

But this, dear one, was Timothy's situation, and the apostle Paul was the "someone" who had asked Timothy to tackle the people *and* the problems in the church at Ephesus.

Evidently Paul had previously purposed to return to Ephesus, but was delayed. Therefore he wrote these instructions about how Timothy and the members of the Ephesian

9

church should conduct themselves in the church and about how they should be growing in their understanding of "the mystery of godliness" (1 Timothy 3:16)—Jesus Christ.

The book of 1 Timothy blesses us with many wonderful themes and lessons. First and foremost (and the major theme), 1 Timothy brims with advice concerning the keys to a successful church (1 Timothy 3:15). It's also filled with personal advice to Timothy from his mentor and father-in-the-faith, Paul. And, as I mentioned above, it offers plenty of advice on godliness. Paul gives us much practical advice, beginning right away in this first lesson.

Let's begin now by receiving a firsthand lesson from the great apostle Paul about *how* to encourage others to continue on in their difficult situations. Read...and revel in...Paul's uplifting, refreshing, opening words of greeting and blessings to young Timothy—words that are, in themselves, most encouraging.

1 Timothy 1:1-2

¹ Paul, an apostle of Jesus Christ, by the commandment of God our Savior and the Lord Jesus Christ, our hope,

² To Timothy, my true son in the faith: Grace, mercy, and peace from God our Father and Jesus Christ our Lord.

Out of God's Word...

Two verses of Scripture! Don't underestimate them, for they are literally *loaded* with truth, facts, people, theology, and encouragement! Let's look now at this pair of verses and consider the four persons mentioned...and be encouraged.

1. First we meet *Paul*. What title did he give himself, and who did he represent (verse 1)?

   an apostle   *God*

   How was Paul given this title (verse 1)?

   by the commandment God and the Lord

2. Next we learn about some of the characteristics of *God*. How is God described...

   ...in verse 1?   ...in verse 2?

   our saviour   *our Lord*

3. Now we learn about some of the characteristics of *Jesus*. How was Jesus described...

   ...in verse 1?   ...in verse 2?

   our hope   *our Lord*

4. Finally, we are introduced to *Timothy*. How was he addressed by Paul in verse 2?

   as a true son

   What do you learn about Timothy from Acts 16:1-3?

   his mother was a Jewess his father a Gentile

   And from 2 Timothy 1:5?

   Paul was low his mother and grandmother were in the faith

   And from 2 Timothy 3:15?

   Paul was taught and learned from a early age the scriptures

5. What three words of greeting and blessing did Paul extend to Timothy (verse 2)?

   Grace, mercy, + peace to Timothy from Paul

   And what was the source of these blessings (verse 2)?

   from God and Jesus Christ our Lord

...and into Your Heart

- *Paul, an apostle*—The term "apostle" means "one who is sent forth." In its specific sense, the title "apostle" speaks of the 12 especially chosen disciples of Christ and of Paul. However, in its general meaning, "apostle" refers to *any* gospel messenger, *any*one who is sent on a spiritual mission, *any*one who brings the message of salvation.[2]

So...do you see yourself as "one who is sent forth" as a gospel messenger? Do you consider that one purpose of your life is that of being on a spiritual mission? Explain your answers.

the world around us is lost and we who know Christ are to be witnesses for him

And...who are the people God has placed in your path who need to hear the message of salvation? Are you a mother or grandmother with a "little Timothy"? Think through your roles at home, church, work, school, in your family, neighborhood, and community, and then jot down the names of those to whom God has sent you forth.

family, friends, neighbor's, colleagues spouse,

- *God our Savior*—The expression "God our Savior" reveals that God is the ultimate source and fountain of our salvation.

- *Jesus our hope*—Delight yourself in these devotional thoughts about our Jesus and our hope...

What a blessed realization is the truth that Christ Jesus is "our hope." Not only that He gives us hope, but He *is* our hope. He is the hope of the individual and of the world; personally, nationally, and internationally. He is our hope in every sense of the term, the object, the author, the foundation, the substance of our hope.[3]

* *Timothy as a faithful son*—Do you have a "Paul" in your life? Someone who was faithful to share the gospel message with you, to train you, and disciple you? This someone could be a parent, a youth leader, a pastor, a seasoned woman, even a peer who's encouraged you to grow in godliness. Have you continued to be faithful to the teaching imparted to you by this faithful servant of God? Part 1 of your assignment is to answer this question honestly and to determine if there are any changes you need to make in your quest for godliness.

And here's Part 2: Why not write or phone this special person God has given to you as a gift? Let her experience the great joy of hearing that you, her child, her "true *daughter* in the faith," are continuing to walk in the truth (3 John 3-4). This is one sure way to encourage those who encourage you!

Heart Response

Because of his faithfulness to Paul and to Paul's teachings, Timothy was a blessing to Paul. But now, as we draw the curtain on these two rich verses, Paul turns around and blesses Timothy by reminding Timothy of the splendid blessings that God the Father and Jesus Christ our Lord continue to lavish upon him. We'll address some of the difficulties the young pastor Timothy faced in the Ephesian church in our next lesson. But, from Word One, from the very opening of his letter, Paul wanted his Timothy to know that he (Timothy) was going into battle with three powerful resources given to him from both God the Father and the Lord Jesus Christ—their grace, their mercy, and their peace.

The same is true for you and me, too, dear one. Whatever we face, whatever the difficulty, the trial, the sorrow, the trouble, the problem, the pain, or the misfortune, we face the foe with the same mighty fortress of God's grace, mercy, and peace.

So…are you encouraged?

esson 2

Watching Out for
False Teachers

1 Timothy 1:3-11

One of my favorite descriptions and pictures of the Proverbs 31 Woman is that of her *watching* over her family and home—"She *watches* over the ways of her household" (Proverbs 31:27, emphasis added). As wives and mothers and homemakers, we women wear many hats as we discharge our duties at home. And there's no doubt that one of our most important duties is that of a "watchwoman." Just as the walls of the ancient cities were dotted with watchmen who guarded the town 24 hours a day against any hostile action, we, too, faithfully and carefully guard our children from harmful influences and sound a warning to our husbands when we feel the family is threatened!

Paul watched, too…over the churches under his charge. In fact, when Paul listed his sufferings for the cause of Christ in 2 Corinthians 11:22-28, he ended his list by stating that "besides the other things, what comes upon me daily: my deep concern for all the churches" (verse 28). Ephesus (as you'll see below) was one of those churches about which Paul had a deep concern. So much so that he had left Timothy behind to carry on what he, Paul, had begun. And now he urges Timothy, too, to watch and to warn.

Before we look into the Scriptures for this lesson, take a minute to familiarize yourself with the stages in the emergence of the church at Ephesus:

Stage 1: Paul preached one time in Ephesus, leaving Aquila and Priscilla there to begin the work of planting a church (Acts 18:19).

Stage 2: Paul returned to Ephesus for several years to preach and minister to an established group of believers (Acts 19).

Stage 3: While at Miletus, Paul met with the leaders of the Ephesian church (Acts 20:17-38), warning them against false teachers before he traveled on to Jerusalem.

Stage 4: Paul wrote the epistle to the Ephesians while imprisoned in Rome (between A.D. 60 and 62).

Stage 5: Paul and Timothy traveled to Ephesus to further instruct the believers against ungodliness and false teaching (1 Timothy 1:3).

Stage 6: Paul left Timothy in Ephesus to carry on the ministry (1 Timothy 1:3).

Stage 7: Paul wrote the epistle of 1 Timothy (between A.D. 62 and 64) to exhort and encourage Timothy in that ministry (1 Timothy 3:14-15).

While this is just a thumbnail account of the six to eight years it took for the magnificent and exciting history of this vibrant, flagship church at Ephesus to unfold, I think it's helpful to have a framework as we study 1 Timothy. Now let's learn more about watching and warning as taught by Paul to Timothy, a fellow watchman.

1 Timothy 1:3-11

³ As I urged you when I went into Macedonia—remain in Ephesus that you may charge some that they teach no other doctrine,

⁴ nor give heed to fables and endless genealogies, which cause disputes rather than godly edification which is in faith.

⁵ Now the purpose of the commandment is love from a pure heart, from a good conscience, and from sincere faith,

⁶ from which some, having strayed, have turned aside to idle talk,

⁷ desiring to be teachers of the law, understanding neither what they say nor the things which they affirm.

⁸ But we know that the law is good if one uses it lawfully,

⁹ knowing this: that the law is not made for a righteous person, but for the lawless and insubordinate, for the ungodly and for sinners, for the unholy and profane, for murderers of fathers and murderers of mothers, for manslayers,

¹⁰ for fornicators, for sodomites, for kidnappers, for liars, for perjurers, and if there is any other thing that is contrary to sound doctrine,

¹¹ according to the glorious gospel of the blessed God which was committed to my trust.

Out of God's Word...

1. What did Paul instruct Timothy to do while Paul was away (verse 3)?

2. Contrast the outcomes of false teaching and true teaching (verse 4).

3. Look at verses 3-7 and give a description of the false teachers.

   They were teaching (verse 3) _____.

   They were giving heed to (verse 4) _____.

   They were causing (verse 4) _____.

   They had (verse 6) _____ and _____ to idle talk.

   They were desiring (verse 7) _____.

   They did not understand (verse 7) what they were _____ or what they _____.

4. The false teachers in Ephesus misunderstood the proper use of the law in the church. Paul sets about to clarify its proper usefulness—the law is not meant for the good person, for the *righteous* person (verse 9), but for the *unrighteous* person (verses 9-10), to show them their sin and bring them to God. What does Galatians 3:24 say about the purpose of the law?

...and into Your Heart

This is quite a passage of Scripture, isn't it? Filled as it is with false teachers, false doctrine, and faulty people, all can seem futile and depressing. However, even in the midst of such darkness, we do find light, "glorious" light! Something positive definitely shines here amidst the negative. False teaching produces the ugliness and evil of ungodliness, but true teaching, sound teaching, produces the beautiful quality of godliness in the life of a church and its people. Before we move on in our exercise, don't fail to notice the brilliance of three bright stars!

- Godly edification—Sound teaching furthers the plan of God (verse 4).

- Good fruit—Sound teaching comes from the heart of a sincere teacher (verse 5).

- Glorious gospel—Sound teaching showcases the glory of God (verse 11).

Now let's put what we've been studying to practical use, remembering that our purpose in studying 1 Timothy is *the pursuit of godliness*.

After reading verses 3-11, I hope you can now recognize the characteristics and behaviors that mark out a false teacher. Now list some of the traits of a teacher of the truth from verses 4, 5, and 11, and then enjoy this beautiful description of such godly teachers.

*S*upposedly there is a cathedral in Venice—the
Cathedral of St. Mark—a marvelous building,
lustrous with an Oriental splendor far beyond
description. There are pillars...of alabaster, a
substance firm and durable as granite, and yet transparent, so that the light glows through them.
Behold an emblem of what all true pillars of the
Church should be—firm in their faith, and
transparent in their character; men of simple mould,
ignorant of tortuous and deceptive ways, and yet
men of strong will, not readily to be led aside or
bent from their uprightness.[4]

Heart Response

Dear reading sister, there is most definitely a need for you
and me, as women after God's own heart, to know the truth!
We *must* be learning, growing, and understanding the doctrines of the Christian faith. We *must* be studying the Bible,
taking classes, and memorizing Scripture. Like the following
story points out, we must make sure we are handling
enough of the *real* thing so that we will recognize the *wrong*
thing when it comes along!

*T*he American Banking Association once sponsored a two-week training program to help tellers detect counterfeit bills. The program was unique—never during the two-week training did the tellers even look at a counterfeit bill, nor did they listen to any lectures concerning the characteristics of counterfeit bills or denouncing the manufacture of counterfeit bills. All they did for two weeks was handle authentic currency, hour after hour and day after day, until they were so familiar with the true that they could not possible be fooled by the false.[5]

So…how can you familiarize yourself with that which is true teaching so that you won't be fooled by the false?

> **W**-ant to be with God's people.
> **A**-sk God for discernment.
> **T**-ake in God's Word.
> **C**-arefully select a Bible-teaching church.
> **H**-eed the warnings of Scripture.

esson 3

Giving Thanks for God's Mercy

1 Timothy 1:12-17

I love Sunday nights at our church! It's such an enlightening time. Why? Because that's when we baptize new believers. How blessed we are to hear the wonderful testimonies of those who have been delivered from the power of darkness and translated into the kingdom of God's glorious light (Colossians 1:12-13)!

Yes, I love Sunday nights at our church because, after a long, hard week (and knowing that another long, hard week awaits me the very next day), it's so invigorating...so inspiring...so heavenly...to bask in the divine experience of saved sinners giving thanks to God for His mercy.

Well, my friend, like a comet streaking across a black sky at night, this next uplifting section of testimony and praise from the heart of Paul, comes to us right on the heels of the dark, dismal facts about false teachers (1 Timothy 1:3-11). You're truly in for a treat as Paul's testimony of his own salvation shows us the difference between "the glorious gospel of the blessed God" (1 Timothy 1:11) and the nothingness of false doctrine. Read on…and see for yourself.

1 Timothy 1:12-17

¹² And I thank Christ Jesus our Lord who has enabled me, because He counted me faithful, putting me into the ministry,

¹³ although I was formerly a blasphemer, a persecutor, and an insolent man; but I obtained mercy because I did it ignorantly in unbelief.

¹⁴ And the grace of our Lord was exceedingly abundant, with faith and love which are in Christ Jesus.

¹⁵ This is a faithful saying and worthy of all acceptance, that Christ Jesus came into the world to save sinners, of whom I am chief.

¹⁶ However, for this reason I obtained mercy, that in me first Jesus Christ might show all long-suffering, as a pattern to those who are going to believe on Him for everlasting life.

¹⁷ Now to the King eternal, immortal, invisible, to God who alone is wise, be honor and glory forever and ever. Amen.

Out of God's Word…

1. Paul begins the testimony of his own pursuit of godliness in verse 12. First he gives thanks. To whom and why?

What else does Paul say about Jesus Christ (verse 15)?

2. Paul was always thankful for God's "grace." How does he describe it here in verse 14?

And in Ephesians 2:8-9?

3. Next, in verse 13, Paul reveals a little about "his past." What kind of person was he?

How does Paul describe all believers before they experience salvation…

…in Ephesians 2:1-3?

…And in Titus 3:3?

4. The letter of 1 Timothy was written toward the end of Paul's life. Look up the following verses and note Paul's words of self-appraisal. Do you detect a pattern as Paul matures in his understanding of godliness?

1 Corinthians 15:9 (written in A.D. 56)—

Ephesians 3:8 (written in A.D. 61)—

1 Timothy 1:15 (written in A.D. 63)—

5. Using words poured out of a heart that "beats with the pulse of the psalmist,"[6] Paul launches into a rich doxology of praise. Clearly, God received all the praise for saving Paul. List the four attributes or characteristics of God that Paul gives thanks for (verse 17).

…and into Your Heart

- *Salvation*—Paul never "got over" his salvation…and neither should we! As you reflect back upon your own salvation experience, what words from 1 Timothy 1:13-16 describe God's work in your life?

- *Strength*—Paul thanked Jesus Christ for His enablement, or His strength (verse 12). How did Paul refer to this same strength and enablement in Philippians 4:13?

- *Service*—Christ not only saves us, but He strengthens and enables us for service. What was Paul's service (verse 12)?

  Now, what are some ways *you* can put God's salvation and strength to work in service according to:

  1 Timothy 3:11?

  1 Timothy 5:10?

  Titus 2:3?

  Can you think of others?

Heart Response

Wow! I know my heart is overflowing with gratitude to God and Christ Jesus for His "exceedingly abundant" grace (verse 14)! With these words Paul expressed the fact that God's grace is "super abundant," more than adequate for all of our sins!

Why don't we do as Paul did? Why don't we make Paul's response our response? Why don't we, too, give thanks to God for His mercy? Why don't we, too, right this minute, burst forth in a doxology? A doxology is a praising, the giving of praise, the expression of glory to God. Spend time now in your own personal outpouring of praise and glory to God. (You may also want to write it out. And don't forget to share it with others!)

Then enjoy the words another woman after God's own heart wrote and shares with us in an old familiar hymn:

Beneath the Cross of Jesus

And from my smitten heart with tears,
Two wonders I confess:
The wonders of redeeming love
And my unworthiness.

Elizabeth C. Clephane

Lesson 4

Exhorting Young Timothy

I'm not really a football fan. However, because of growing up with my three brothers...and my dad (who had played college football)...and living with my husband, Jim...and also having two sons-in-law, I am somewhat familiar with the game! (Probably every woman is "somewhat familiar" with football, whether she wants to be or not!) Anyway, I've seen the huddles where the calls are made, the game-plays are determined, and the players are spurred on.

Well, today I want you to imagine such a huddle...a huddle of two. The pair is made up of the seasoned coach—the apostle Paul, and the young player—timid Timothy. Perhaps with his arm affectionately around the young pastor

Timothy's shoulders, the aged Paul gives Timothy a few words of exhortation and some helpful advice on how to handle the battles he was encountering at Ephesus.

Do you need some encouragement, my friend? Do you need a little advice for handling your difficult situations? Then draw close, lean near, and listen in on the huddle.

1 Timothy 1:18-20

18 This charge I commit to you, son Timothy, according to the prophecies previously made concerning you, that by them you may wage the good warfare,

19 having faith and a good conscience, which some having rejected, concerning the faith have suffered shipwreck,

20 of whom are Hymenaeus and Alexander, whom I delivered to Satan that they may learn not to blaspheme.

Out of God's Word...

As you examine these few verses of Scripture, you'll notice that Paul's words seem to fall into two categories—personal advice to Timothy and pastoral advice regarding false teachers.

1. *Personal advice*—With what words does Paul begin his exhortation (verse 18)?

For your information...Paul's reference to "this charge" (1 Timothy 1:18) points back to 1 Timothy 1:3 and 5, where Timothy was commanded to promote sound doctrine by prohibiting false teachers and their doctrines.

And what terms of endearment does he use toward Timothy (verse 18)?

What event does Paul remind Timothy of that should strengthen him for fulfilling his duty in the Ephesian church (verse 18)?

(Again, for your information…"according to the prophecies" probably refers to Timothy's commissioning service where the elders most likely laid hands on him, set him apart for ministry, and affirmed his spiritual giftedness and ability for the ministry.

And what was the duty Timothy was to fulfill (verse 18)?

What two spiritual necessities must Timothy hold on to in order to wage a successful military campaign (verse 19)?

2. *Pastoral advice*—Not all were as faithful as Timothy! What demise did "some" suffer (verse 19)?

Paul names names. Who were two false teachers that came to his mind (verse 20)?

And what action had Paul taken against them (verse 20)?

And why (verse 20)?

The phrase "delivered to Satan" probably referred to church discipline exercised only by apostles such as Paul. (For another instance, see 1 Corinthians 5:1-5.) By putting "blasphemers" out of the church and outside the spiritual protection of the church, hopefully the erring ones would come to their senses and be restored to fellowship in the church.

...and into Your Heart

Paul used two images in exhorting Timothy.

* *A Christian must be a good "soldier."* Paul encouraged Timothy to "wage the good warfare" (verse 18). Paul is not referring to a single battle, but to a whole military campaign. First of all, do you consider yourself engaged in warfare? What does Paul say in Ephesians 6:12 about your life as a Christian?

  What is Paul's exhortation to us in Ephesians 6:10 as we engage in spiritual warfare?

  According to Ephesians 6:11 and 13, what has God given to us as Christians for fighting this battle?

  Like Timothy, we, too, must maintain a hold on "faith and a good conscience." We must cling tightly to our faith, refuse to give in to temptation, and live out our faith with a clear conscience.

How can you hold on to a good conscience? Treasure your faith in Christ more than anything else and do what you know is right. Each time you deliberately ignore your conscience, you are hardening your heart. Over a period of time your capacity to tell right from wrong will diminish. As you walk with God, he will speak to you through your conscience, letting you know the difference between right and wrong. Be sure to act on those inner tugs so that you do what is right—then your conscience will remain clear.[7]

Now it's time to personalize Paul's message to Timothy. Is the Holy Spirit sounding any warning to your conscience about some aspect of your behavior? Are you doing what you know is right? Or are you deliberately ignoring some inner tug from your conscience and hardening your heart? Take some time to reflect on these tough-but-important questions.

What solution does 1 John 1:9 offer for any sin issues that come to mind?

And what does Psalm 139:23-24 advise when nothing comes to mind?

- *A Christian must be a good "sailor."* In 1 Timothy 1:19, Paul switches from the picture of a military campaign to that of a shipwreck. As this picture has been explained, *"a good conscience*—one that obeys the dictates of the Word as applied to the heart by the Holy Spirit—is the rudder, guiding the believer's vessel into the safe harbor of everlasting rest."[8]

What will help you and me to "navigate" through sin and error?

✓ God's Word—How does God's Word guide us, according to Psalm 119:105?

✓ Prayer—We'll learn more about the importance of prayer in our next lesson, but for now, how can Proverbs 3:6 steer us in the right direction?

✓ Christian fellowship—According to Hebrews 10:23-25, how does close fellowship with other strong believers help us to stand strong and stay on course?

Heart Response

As I look back over this lesson and Paul's exhortation to Timothy, one thing stands out vividly to me. The Christian life is a battle—a *spiritual* battle! We may not like it, and we may wish otherwise, but it's true.

Therefore, we, like Paul and Timothy, must "wage the good warfare." We, too, must cling to two inseparable, invaluable, dispositions of the heart—faith and a good conscience. These words touched my heart and come with a prayer that will also touch yours.

> One's faith and one's morals cannot be separated. To hold tightly to the Christian faith, and live by it, results in a good (peaceful) conscience. Faith and good conscience are like armor for the Christian. They keep us from giving in to temptation and to debilitating spiritual and moral sidetracks....
> Rejecting the faith and refusing to listen to one's conscience will end in destroyed faith.[9]

Now, can you think of any better way to pursue godliness than to ask God to help you keep the faith and keep yourself pure?

Lesson 5

Praying God's Way

*I*magine living in a country where the leaders are not Christians—and, in fact, are becoming hostile to the Christian faith. You've heard reports of hostile acts committed against some of your brothers and sisters in Christ in other cities...and even in your own.

Well, that's what was beginning to take place all over the Roman Empire in the days of 1 Timothy. Leaders across the empire were beginning to take note of Christianity as being non-Jewish and against emperor worship. As a result, they were starting a campaign of persecution against the followers of Jesus Christ.

Now imagine this! In your worship service your pastor asks you to *pray* for these people—the very ones who are

33

oppressing you and your brothers and sisters in Christ!!! How would you respond? *Could* you do it? *Would* you do it?

Before you answer these questions, prayerfully move through this lesson on prayer. And don't forget to ask God to give you a better understanding of praying God's way.

1 Timothy 2:1-8

1 Therefore I exhort first of all that supplications, prayers, intercessions, and giving of thanks be made for all men,

2 for kings and all who are in authority, that we may lead a quiet and peaceable life in all godliness and reverence.

3 For this is good and acceptable in the sight of God our Savior,

4 who desires all men to be saved and to come to the knowledge of the truth.

5 For there is one God and one Mediator between God and men, the Man Christ Jesus,

6 who gave Himself a ransom for all, to be testified in due time,

7 for which I was appointed a preacher and an apostle—I am speaking the truth in Christ and not lying—a teacher of the Gentiles in faith and truth.

8 Therefore I desire that the men pray everywhere, lifting up holy hands, without wrath and doubting;

Out of God's Word...

As we step into chapter 2 of 1 Timothy, note a change in the subject matter of Paul's instructions to Timothy: Paul moves from the general to the specific. Here he turns his attention from the general issues of the church to the specific duties within the church.

1. *What* does Paul see as a primary responsibility of the church (verse 1)?

   What four terms does Paul use for the practice of prayer (verse 1)?

   _____   _____

   _____   _____

2. *Who* are to be the objects of prayer (verses 1-2)?

   What might result from praying for such people (verse 2)?

3. *Why* were believers to engage in such prayer according to...

   ...verse 3?—

   ...verse 4?—

4. What do we learn about God in verse 5?

   And about Jesus in verses 5 and 6?

5. Paul addresses our role as *women* in our next lesson, but here he directs his attention to the *men* and their role as spiritual leaders in prayer in the church. What instructions does he give them (verse 8)?

...and into Your Heart

Paul placed primary importance on prayer in the worship service and begins his specific instructions to Timothy regarding the church by focusing on the *kinds* of prayer the church should be engaged in.

- *Supplications*—Coming from a Greek word meaning "to lack," this kind of prayer occurs because of a need. We have a need; therefore, we make supplication. We request and we petition. "A conscious sense of need is essential to all effective praying."[10]

- *Prayers*—This word is used of prayer to God, implying reverence in prayer.

- *Intercessions*—We can approach God in confident, familiar prayer. Intercessions suggests personal and confiding conversation with God on behalf of others.

- *Giving of thanks*—Thanksgiving is the complement of all true prayer. All of our supplications, prayers, and intercessions are to be offered in the spirit of gratitude.

  Are any of these four aspects lacking in your prayer life, dear one? If so, how can you begin to incorporate them today? This minute?

  The man or woman who pursues godliness is a man or woman who prays. When it comes to praying for the lost (even those who persecute and mistreat us), how should knowing that God desires all men to be saved affect your prayers for others?

Heart Response

Now...back to our opening scenario. Paul was asking the congregation in Ephesus—and us—to pray as a part of their worship service for kings and those in authority who were becoming their enemies. Why should you and I follow these instructions? Because our faithful prayers for the leaders of our country—whether hostile to or supportive of Christianity—can make a difference in their lives, in our country, in our church, and in our lives. Also, our prayers enhance our own personal godliness. It's true that not only does prayer change *things*, but prayer also changes *us!*

So *pray!* Pray for all men. Pray for your governmental officials. Pray for those in authority. And pray for your church. And your friends. And for your enemies and those who hate you and curse you and spitefully use you (Luke 6:27-28).

But, dear woman (and wife and mother and daughter and sister) after God's own heart, especially *pray* fervently for your family! *Give thanks* for those in your family circle who love the Lord Jesus Christ. *Intercede* for your loved ones. But commit yourself to impassioned *supplication* for that husband...or child...or mother or father...or brother or sister...who does not embrace our Savior.

I must share with you something that I heard in a lecture at our church's women's Bible study, an example of a mother who interceded for *her* loved one. In her case, it was her beloved errant son. Please read the testimony of this praying woman's son now (see on the next page). May her commitment to prayer and fervency in prayer stimulate yours!

Augustine, who died in A.D. 430, was one of the greatest and most influential leaders of the western Church. And he was richly and eternally blessed to have a devoted and saintly Christian mother, Monica. In his "confessions," Augustine wrote that "for nine years while I was rolling in the filth of sin, often attempting to rise, and still sinking deeper, did she, in vigorous hope, persist in uncessant prayer. Thy hands, my God, in the secret of Thy providence, forsook not my soul. Day and night the prayers of my mother came up before Thee...."

Monica's life employment was praying for her son. His salvation was the constant burden of her supplication. Shortly after he was saved she told him her reason for living was over, and she died five days later.

Lesson 6

Learning About Your Role

1 Timothy 2:9-15

*T*ake notice, my friend—this may well be the longest lesson in our study. However, it may also be the most important one for us as women who are pursuing godliness! So...let's get to the heart of what it means to be a woman after God's own heart and learn about our role in the home, the church, and in society.

1 Timothy 2:9-15

⁹ in like manner also, that the women adorn themselves in modest apparel, with propriety and moderation, not with braided hair or gold or pearls or costly clothing,

¹⁰ but, which is proper for women professing god-liness, with good works.

¹¹ Let a woman learn in silence with all submis-sion.

¹² And I do not permit a woman to teach or to have authority over a man, but to be in silence.

¹³ For Adam was formed first, then Eve.

¹⁴ And Adam was not deceived, but the woman being deceived, fell into transgression.

¹⁵ Nevertheless she will be saved in childbearing if they continue in faith, love, and holiness, with self-control.

Out of God's Word...

As we approach this passage of Scripture that delivers a major message to us as women, don't forget that Paul is instructing Timothy about what is proper in the worship ser-vice. Having just finished dealing with the attitude with which the *men* were to pray (1 Timothy 2:8), Paul now turns to the subject of the attitude and behavior of the *women*.

1. Here Paul addresses the issue of godliness in Christian women. He begins with *proper* clothing. What is and is not to be the focus of our dress (verse 9)?

   What does Paul say is to be our ultimate *proper* "clothing" (verse 10)?

2. Note Paul's three guidelines regarding a woman's role and conduct in the worship service.

   Verse 11—

Verse 12—

Verse 12—

Next Paul gives the reasons for his guidelines. Write them out, too.

Verse 13—

Verse 14—

3. Paul closes with a positive word about the powerful contribution godly women can make to society, mankind, and the church. Write out verse 15.

...and into Your Heart

As we step into this section reserved for comprehending God's Word and applying it in our hearts and lives, four main points call for our attention. Please remember as you move through them that the first three apply to each and every Christian woman. And, as you'll see, the fourth point shows us the beauty of being a dedicated and godly Christian mother if we have children.

* *Regarding our appearance*—Seven words from Paul's portrait of godliness show us God's "dress code." The first six are as follows:

   —*Adorn* means to arrange, to put in order, or make ready. We get our word *cosmetic* from the Greek word translated "adorn." This verb pictures orderly and proper arrangement as a habitual way of life.

   —*Modest* refers to proper clothing.

—*Propriety* refers to modesty mixed with humility.

—*Moderation* is self-control, especially over sexual passions.

—*Proper* has the idea of order, apparel that is well-arranged and in good taste.

—*Godliness* means reverence to God; therefore, women with such godly reverence should display it by their demeanor, their appearance, and by their good works.

Look at 1 Peter 3:3-4. What does Peter say is more important to God than our clothing and appearance?

Paul is not saying that it's wrong to look nice! Describe the attire of the woman of Proverbs 31:22.

Don't miss Paul's point to Timothy (and us!): A woman cannot claim to fear God and yet disregard what God says about her behavior, her appearance, and her ministry.

What conclusions can you draw and what changes can you make regarding your appearance?

- *Regarding our conduct*—Paul puts the finishing touch on his picture of a godly woman with a seventh word— women are to adorn themselves with that which is proper for women professing godliness, "with *good works*" (1 Timothy 2:9-10, emphasis added). *Good works* is the positive adornment that a godly woman prizes most highly.

Make a list of the *good works* detailed for us in 1 Timothy 5:10.

Optional question: Scan Proverbs 31:10-31 and list a few of the "good works" performed by this woman in her home and in her community.

What conclusions can you draw and what changes can you make regarding your conduct?

- *Regarding our role*—Lengthy arguments have been written, both pro and con, by those for and against what Paul states in verse 11 regarding the behavior of women in the church body: "Let a woman learn in silence with all submission." As we continue in our study of *Pursuing Godliness*, let's first do our *homework*, and then pray for God's help in *doing* (as in *living out*) our homework!

  Paul's teaching regarding the role of women in the church is not based on the culture of his day nor on Jewish culture: Instead, Paul points...

    —First, to the order of creation. What does Genesis 2:21-23 say on this subject?

    —Next, to the deception of Eve by Satan. Briefly, what does Genesis 3:1-6 reveal?

- Also consider the teaching of 1 Corinthians 11:8-9.

  Just a note: Paul's command has nothing to do with a woman's *spiritual* position. Look up Galatians 3:28 and write out its teaching. Then read the following explanation.

  > The Bible places women in a lofty position equal with men in their standing before Christ. Only when it comes to function (roles) does the Bible make a distinction.

  > Take, for example, a Christian family. God asks the husband to lead, the wife to submit, and the children to obey. All are saved and will spend eternity with Christ, but during their lifetime they are asked by God to fulfill different roles.

  > But the supreme example is Christ and His relationship with the Father during His time on the earth. Jesus Christ modeled perfection...although He was equal with the Father, He took on the role of a servant and was submissive to the Father in all things.

  We should all thank God for the opportunities to submit to His design for godliness and to fulfill the different roles He is asking us to perform, including our roles in the church.

  What conclusions can you draw and what changes can you make regarding your role as a woman in the church?

- *Regarding our parenting*—Obviously, the three categories above apply to all women, single and married, young and old, both to women without children and with children.

However, as we look at this final category, Paul seems to be addressing those who are mothers. Here Paul writes, "...she will be saved in childbearing if they continue in faith, love, and holiness, with self-control." Even though we as women bear the punishment and stigma of Eve's deception and fall, we are saved, or preserved, or freed, from that stigma by raising godly children and living our lives in a godly way.

For an example of a woman (and her mother) who gave the world and the church a godly child, look at 2 Timothy 1:5 and 3:15. What is Paul describing?

All mothers share in the experience of childbearing or childbirth. However, what four graces of Christian character set the Christian woman apart and contribute to her influence in the home, church, and society (1 Timothy 2:15)?

For most women, their greatest impact on society is through raising godly children. If a woman is godly and if God chooses to give her children whom she raises in the nurture and admonition of the Lord, she will have a profound influence on a new generation. Men may have the outward, overt leadership, but women may have just as great an influence indirectly.[11]

What conclusions can you draw and what changes can you make regarding your privilege and responsibility as a mother, if God has given you that role?

Finally, what encouragement can you take away from this lesson?

Heart Response

Congratulations on making it through this lesson! (And I hope you agree that this was a crucial one!) The book of 1 Timothy places much emphasis on pursuing godliness, on actively striving for a reverential heart attitude that is shown in our actions. And I'm sure you agree that we as women after God's own heart cannot claim to reverence and worship God and, at the same time, disregard what He says about our behavior and our roles.

So, from my heart to yours, here's what I (and Paul and God's Word) want for you and me, dear sister. Rather than struggling and wrangling over the issues of teaching or silence or submission in the church, we as women pursuing godliness should set our hearts and minds and efforts to work on showing forth, by our ministry of good works—in the church and with our family at home—the reality of God's salvation in our lives.

God *will* bless us as we pursue godliness in these ways!

esson 7

Instructing Church Leaders

*I*t's often been said, "Aim at nothing and you will hit it every time." And it's true! Goals and standards generally ensure progress. Knowing where you are going (or should be going!) means you will probably get there...or at least move in the intended direction.

Well, my friend, *godliness* is a goal and a desire for every woman after God's own heart to pursue. And God has just shared with us some of His glorious guidelines for our conduct and service in the church.

And now God gives us His standards and instructions for the men who desire to serve in leadership in the church, instructions that most definitely involve pursuing a life of godliness!

47

1 Timothy 3:1-7

¹ This is a faithful saying: If a man desires the position of a bishop, he desires a good work.

² A bishop then must be blameless, the husband of one wife, temperate, sober-minded, of good behavior, hospitable, able to teach;

³ not given to wine, not violent, not greedy for money, but gentle, not quarrelsome, not covetous;

⁴ one who rules his own house well, having his children in submission with all reverence

⁵ (for if a man does not know how to rule his own house, how will he take care of the church of God?);

⁶ not a novice, lest being puffed up with pride he fall into the same condemnation as the devil.

⁷ Moreover he must have a good testimony among those who are outside, lest he fall into reproach and the snare of the devil.

Out of God's Word...

1. As Paul heads into this section of instructions for church leaders, what encouraging "saying" does he begin with (verse 1)?

2. Next Paul notes the moral qualities required of a "bishop" (verses 2-3). List them here.

The words *bishop, elder, overseer,* and *pastor* are used interchangeably in the New Testament. For an example, see Acts 20:17,28. For our purposes, we'll use the term "overseer."

3. In verses 2 and 4, Paul addresses an overseer's relationship with his family. Describe that relationship here.

Why is an overseer's home life important to his service in the church (verse 5)?

4. Paul continues: According to verse 3, what should an overseer's attitude toward money be?

And why does Paul say spiritual maturity is important in an overseer (verse 6)?

Furthermore, what should an overseer's reputation be in his community (verse 7)?

...and into Your Heart

• *As a Christian*—Every Christian—man or woman—*should* seek to possess the godly, moral qualities Paul lists in verses 2 and 3. (Indeed, most of them are commanded in the Bible for all believers.) But Paul says that an overseer or an elder *must* possess them! Read verses 2 and 3 again. Did any of the characteristics of godliness speak to your heart? Which ones were they? And why?

Are there any behaviors or attitudes named in verses 2 and 3 that you need to work on in your life? And how will you go about doing that?

- *As a wife*—Did you notice how many of the qualifications for a church leader point to a vital joint role with his wife (if he has one)? I counted at least four. She is to be…

  …a faithful wife (verse 2). What do these scriptures teach us about the role of a faithful wife?

    Genesis 2:18—

    Ephesians 5:22-24—

    Ephesians 5:33—

    Titus 2:4—

  And what does Proverbs 31:11-12 say about a faithful wife?

  …a friend of strangers (verse 2)—Hospitality means "stranger love." And as a book title puts it, we are to have an *Open Heart, Open Home*.[12] What did the worthy women in 1 Timothy 5:10 do to demonstrate their open hearts and open homes to those in need?

  …a follower of her husband's leadership (verse 4)—Look again at Ephesians 5:22-24 and Colossians 3:18. How do we demonstrate our faithful following of our husband's leadership?

  …a fantastic mom (verse 4)—A godly mother and father should form a godly team committed to the godly training of godly children. Whether Dad is in the house or not,

what instructions does Deuteronomy 6:6-7 give you as a godly mother?

Whether your husband is a church leader or not, how can you be more helpful in your role as a wife in the above four areas? (Now, why not go the extra mile and discuss this with your husband?)

Heart Response

I don't know what kind of father Charles Spurgeon was, but based on the following story I think we can learn a little about what kind of wife and mother *Mrs.* Spurgeon was. Susannah Spurgeon was married to this man who was the famed preacher of London's Metropolitan Tabernacle. Spurgeon's ministry was thriving, but he became concerned that he might be neglecting his children. So Charles Spurgeon returned home earlier than usual one evening. Opening the door, he was surprised to find none of the children in the hall. Ascending the stairs, he heard his wife's voice and knew that she was engaged in prayer with the children. One by one she named the children in prayer. When she finished her prayer and her nightly instructions to their little ones, Spurgeon thought, "I can go on with my work. My children are well cared for."[13]

Does this faithful woman's care of her home and family help you to understand…just a little better…how we who are wives and mothers can make a positive contribution to our husband's life and ministry?

Lesson 8

Obtaining God's Reward

1 Timothy 3:8-13

I'm proud ("Christian" proud, that is) of my wonderful husband, Jim, for a lifetime of many, many wonderful qualities and accomplishments. And recently I had the privilege of being proud of him one more time. To make a long story short, Jim has faithfully served as a pharmacy officer in the U.S. Army Reserves for more than 20 years (in addition to being a husband, father, provider, minister, and professor). His crowning feat for the Army was activation for five months in Germany during one of our country's recent overseas crises.

Finally it was time for Jim to retire from the Army Reserves. In standard military fashion, we as a family were invited to his retirement ceremony. So off Jim and I went—along with our daughter Katherine, her husband, Paul, and their baby, Taylor Jane—down to the West Coast training center in Los Alamitos, California.

Well, because I had never been to one of these spectacles before, I was in no way prepared for the magnitude of the occasion. A full military band was performing, marching, and presenting the flags. The soldiers were decked out in dress uniforms. A two-star general's helicopter landed on the adjacent field, bringing him in for the ceremony to personally pin on medals and award certificates signed by the president of the United States. (Jim wasn't the only one to be recognized.) The retiring soldiers were decorated, speeches were made, wives were honored, and a sit-down dinner crowned the celebration.

Yes, as I said, I was proud—*very* proud! All of this honor was awarded to Jim because of one thing—faithful service.

Even though receiving awards and rewards is never to be a motive for faithfulness, church leaders, too, can and should receive recognition for their faithful service. Read now what Paul tells Timothy about the rewards of being spiritually mature men who faithfully "serve as deacons."

1 Timothy 3:8-13

⁸ Likewise deacons must be reverent, not double-tongued, not given to much wine, not greedy for money,

⁹ holding the mystery of the faith with a pure conscience.

¹⁰ But let these also first be proved; then let them serve as deacons, being found blameless....

¹² Let deacons be the husbands of one wife, ruling their children and their own houses well.

> [13] For those who have served well as deacons
> obtain for themselves a good standing and great
> boldness in the faith which is in Christ Jesus.

Out of God's Word...

1. In this passage of Scripture, Paul moves on from the over-seers in our previous lesson to the second office in the church. What are these men called (verse 8)?

2. Take a minute and read 1 Timothy 3:1-7 again. Compare the two passages and list the qualities that are different for deacons in verses 8-13 from those of a bishop/elder (verses 1-7).

   As a side note, what are the two groups of leaders recognized by Paul in Philippians 1:1?

3. What are the two domestic qualifications for deacons (verse 12)?

   How do these domestic qualifications correspond to the domestic standards set for the bishops/elders in verses 4-5?

4. Now record the two rewards for faithful service mentioned in verse 13.

5. What is the deacon's bold faith based on (verse 13)?

...and into Your Heart

I'm sure you noticed that we skipped verse 11. We'll look at that special verse for women in our next lesson. But for now, this lesson is about the group of men in the church who serve as deacons. I especially love this passage because once a year I receive a letter from my church that is sent out to every church member announcing that it's once again time to nominate deacons for the next calendar year. And these very verses are in the letter! So, as a woman, these verses are important to me (and you, too!) because they spell out God's guidelines for such leaders. This helps me to recognize such men and appreciate them for their character.

- First we need a definition of a deacon. Pure and simple, he is one who obeys the commands of another, a servant. He serves alongside the bishops/elders of the church, assisting in the serving aspects of ministry.

- Many Bible experts see the beginning of the office of deacon in Acts 6:1-5. Read this exciting story now. What was the problem and what triggered it (Acts 6:1)?

  And what was the solution (verse 3)?

  Describe the kind of men who were chosen for this task (verse 3).

  What similarities do you notice in Acts 6:3 and 1 Timothy 3:13?

- This lesson is titled "Obtaining God's Reward," and 1 Timothy 3:13 mentions two rewards:

  Reward #1—A good standing. The phrase "good standing," in Paul's day as well as ours, speaks of community respect, as this scholar explains:

  > Paul is not speaking of the ecclesiastical advancement of the deacon to the overseership, nor is he speaking of the future reward in glory. The reference is to the

excellent community standing and recognition which they acquire through their having rendered good service.[14]

Reward #2—Great boldness in the faith. When a leader faithfully discharges his duties and constantly strives to meet the qualifications of a deacon (and this applies to the bishops/elders from lesson 7 as well), he will have the personal integrity to speak boldly—and brilliantly!—as a representative of Jesus Christ to those who are lost in a dark world.

Summed up, Paul says that faithful service will result in the reward of recognition both by the church *and* by the community, both by believers *and* unbelievers. His character of life will provide a platform to share his faith boldly.

And now for you, dear woman after God's own heart! What one area of your life can you start improving today so that in the years to come your godliness will benefit others and be a beacon of light in a dark world? Don't just name the area(s). Put some feet on it by mapping out a plan to move out into specific actions.

Heart Response

Deacons, dear reader, are *required* to be faithful. Faithfulness is a high calling, and you and I as women should *desire* to be faithful too (as we'll see in our next lesson), not for the recognition that it might bring to us personally, but to our Savior, the Lord Jesus.

Also, deacons who serve faithfully in their role of leadership will have their rewards. And we will have our rewards, too, if we serve well in our arenas of service. Faithfulness is not made up of any one heroic act. No, it's an everyday occurrence. So let's quietly...and faithfully...go about the everyday business of serving others in our roles...

> *...as wives.* If you are married, make sure you live out that biblical role so that your husband's good standing is enhanced...and not endangered!

> *...as mothers.* If God has blessed you with children, set about to faithfully fulfill that responsibility as a godly mother.

When these two roles are owned and faithfully pursued, one of our rewards may be *praise*, as was true of the Proverbs 31 Woman, who enjoyed the praise of her children (Proverbs 31:28), her husband (verses 28 and 29), and of others (verse 31).

> *...as workers in the church.* Well, let's move on to our next study to discover the beauty—and rewards—of faithful service in the church!

Lesson 9

Ministering Faithfully

1 Timothy 3:11

I especially love this one verse in Paul's first letter to Timothy. It's about the role *of* women in the church *to* women in the church. In my home church, women involved in this ministry are called *deaconesses*, and it's been my privilege to serve in this capacity for more than 20 years.

I well remember doing a little research on this special group of women when I was first asked to join their ranks. It seems that, as the early church grew, new needs arose. Who, for instance, would teach the new female believers? Who would counsel them regarding marriage and family problems? Who would tend to them in childbirth, illness, destitution, and death? Who would visit them in their homes? Who would guide them through the baptism ceremony?

In answer to these special needs, a special group of women was called upon to help the women in the church with such works of charity. What kind of women were they? Let's find out, because they set the standard for you and me, too.

1 *Timothy* 3:11

¹¹ Likewise their wives must be reverent, not slanderers, temperate, faithful in all things.

Out of God's Word...

1. First a quick look backward—What groups of men in the church have we studied so far in...

   ...1 Timothy 3:1-7?

   ...1 Timothy 3:8-10 and 12-13?

   As we turn now to verse 11, we encounter the word *likewise*. Of whom was this word used in verse 8?

2. What group does Paul now address in verse 11?

   In case you're wondering about the word *wives*, there's no doubt that it's a convenient arrangement when a husband and wife each qualify as deacon and deaconess and can serve in the church as a couple. Therefore, some scholars and church leaders do not see this woman as anything other than the wife of a deacon. But it's also true that the Greek word rendered *wives* can also be *women*. Here Paul could be referring, *not* to deacons' wives, but to the women who serve as female deacons, or deaconesses.

Record the four behaviors that qualify these women for ministry (verse 11).

_____   _____

_____   _____

3. Now read back through verses 1-10 and note the similarities in qualifications for these three groups of officials in the church—overseers, deacons, and deaconesses.

...and into Your Heart

In my devotional book *Women Who Loved God,*[15] I designated four readings to describing the role of deaconess in the church and the four qualities that set up a woman in leadership as a role model for the women she serves. Let's take a closer look at those four qualities now.

- *Reverent and dignified*—Since God is first and foremost in the heart of every woman who pursues godliness, hers is a life of worship. This woman lives in the presence of the God she loves, and that position gives her actions dignity and decorum. As a daughter of the King, she acts with a certain nobility and regality. Her devotion to God is evident in all that she says and does, and there is a seriousness and purpose to her life which cannot be missed.

  How does Titus 2:3 describe the godly "older women" in the church?

  Does your behavior reflect a certain godly dignity that invites the respect of other people? Does your conduct reflect something of the majesty of the Lord? When others have contact with you, do they sense that you are a dignitary for Deity? If not, what behaviors do you need to eliminate...or include...in your daily walk with the Lord?

• *Not slanderers*—A person who talks maliciously about others is called a gossip—a word used in the Bible for the devil himself. His very name is *diabolos*, "slanderer." In fact, "slanderer" is used 34 times in Scripture as a title for Satan and once to refer to Judas, the one who betrayed our Jesus (John 6:70). This is frightening company! The two extremes—helping women by our works and hurting women by our words—just do not go together!

What can you do today—now!—to eliminate gossip from your life? Name at least five things you can do.

*J*ust as a young doctor pledges in the Hippocratic oath never to repeat anything that he has heard from or about a patient, so the woman God uses is not to repeat anything she sees or hears about the women God calls her to help.

P.S.—What practical advice does Titus 3:2 give us for overcoming the problem of slander?

- *Temperate*—God's high calling to physical temperance was originally issued to women in a culture where drunkenness was a way of life. Temperance is more than a call to abstain from alcoholic excess. It's also an emotional calling to be calm and dispassionate, grave and sober. It's a call to self-control in all areas of life. Women who serve in the church are to be free from excesses in and addiction to anything!

  Look at how Daniel handled temptation in Daniel 1:5-8. Then note specifically how you can set about to follow in his faithful footsteps.

- *Faithful in all things*—A female servant in the church must also be absolutely reliable and completely trustworthy as she carries out the business of the church. She must faithfully live out her love of Christ as she faithfully performs her God-given duties according to the instructions she receives. Truly a faithful-in-all-things woman is a blessing to the church body.

  What principle for faithfulness does Luke 16:10 give us?

  And 1 Corinthians 4:2?

  Now read Titus 2:4-5 and make a list of some areas that call for great faithfulness that may, at first glance, appear to be "little things" but are actually "big things" to God.

  Now list some areas for improvement. (And don't forget to make a plan of action!)

Heart Response

As a woman after God's own heart, is faithfully serving God one of the deep-seated desires of your heart? Faithfulness is not only a beautiful quality in God's women, but it is an important concept in the New Testament. Jesus spoke often of it. The apostle Paul required it of himself and those who ministered with him. The saints in the book of Revelation will have demonstrated it. And here in 1 Timothy, young Timothy exemplified it (1:2).

Take a moment now and ask God to assist you in your everyday life to be "faithful in all things." No matter how big (public service in the church) or small (quiet deeds done at home), you must minister faithfully.

Faithfulness—it's a good thing! And it's a good way to begin...and end...your pursuit of godliness.

Lesson 10

Pursuing Godliness

1 Timothy 3:14-16

ave you ever received a letter from someone important to you and wondered why they sent it? You read it eagerly, searching for words of explanation, but found none. You tried "reading between the lines" but you still couldn't fathom why they wrote the letter.

Well, the apostle Paul definitely did not want this sort of uncertainty to happen with his letter to Timothy (nor with the content of this priceless portion of it!), so he plainly stated its reasons in these verses. I don't think Timothy (or you and I) missed the point—it's about our conduct in the church. It's about Christians pursuing Christlike godliness as we look to Him.

1 Timothy 3:14-16

¹⁴ These things I write to you, though I hope to come to you shortly;

¹⁵ but if I am delayed, I write so that you may know how you ought to conduct yourself in the house of God, which is the church of the living God, the pillar and ground of the truth.

¹⁶ And without controversy great is the mystery of godliness:

> God was manifested in the flesh,
> Justified in the Spirit,
> Seen by angels,
> Preached among the Gentiles,
> Believed on in the world,
> Received up in glory.

Out of God's Word...

1. First, Paul wrote this letter with what possibility (verse 14)?

   In the meantime, however, what did Paul want Timothy to know (verse 15)?

2. How does Paul describe "the house of God" (verse 15)?

3. What indisputable fact is stated in verse 16?

4. Now list the realities of the life of Christ, which Paul labels "the mystery of godliness."

…and into Your Heart

- *Church*—Here Paul speaks of "the church of the living God." When Paul uses this term, he is not speaking of a building. In fact, nowhere in the New Testament does *church* refer to a physical building. Rather it is used of the *people* who make up the church. Note how these references describe God's people as the church:

  1 Corinthians 3:16-17—

  2 Corinthians 6:16—

  Ephesians 2:19-22—

  You, as a member of the church of the living God, according to Paul's beautiful imagery, are a part of the *pillar* and *ground* of the truth. What difference should these facts make in your conduct both in the church and in the community?

- *Christ*—First let's note a few descriptions and definitions to help our understanding:

  A "*mystery*" is a truth that has been hidden in the past but is now revealed.

  "*The* mystery" spoken of here is the divine scheme embodied in Christ, which was once hidden from, but is now revealed to, us who believe.[16]

  How does Colossians 1:27 describe this mystery?

  "The mystery of *godliness*" means that it is now possible for those who believe to live a godly life in and through Jesus Christ. Put plainly and simply, this is *piety*, a deep-seated loyalty and devotion that affects our conduct and commitment to spiritual duties and practices. Now, once again, what difference should these facts make in your conduct both in the church and in the community?

- *Confession*—I dearly love the great time-honored hymns of the faith. And here is a *really* old hymn! Paul now expresses and confesses, in six exquisite lines from an early church hymn that might well be titled "Hymn in Adoration of the Christ,"[17] the core of the gospel and who Jesus Christ is. Let's consider it line upon line, remembering that every phrase of this early hymn is a mystery beyond our ability to comprehend, yet the truths are ours to believe:

  —God was manifested in the flesh. This is an obvious reference to Christ, who revealed the invisible God to mankind. Note John's description of this mystery in John 1:14 and 18.

  —Justified in the Spirit. Here is a declaration of Christ's righteousness based on His sinless life. What do Isaiah 55:3 and Hebrews 13:12 reveal about Christ's acceptance among *men*?

    It was by the *Spirit* that Jesus Christ was justified, and His own perfect righteousness and the validity of His claims were fully established.

  —Seen by angels. It appears that the angels witnessed the entire drama of the Incarnation. For a few instances of these occurrences, note Matthew 4:11, Luke 2:9-14, and Acts 1:10-11.

—Preached among the Gentiles. This phrase points to the worldwide proclamation of the gospel. What is our part in this proclamation according to Matthew 28:18-20?

—Believed on in the world. Christ is not only preached among the nations, but He is also believed on across the world. Describe for yourself the scene in Revelation 5:9-10.

—Received up in glory. As one scholar surmises, "Having been manifested in the flesh, vindicated by the Spirit, seen by angels, and having issued the order which resulted in the proclamation of His name among the nations and the outgathering of a spiritual harvest from the world, He 'was taken up.'"[18] To catch a glimpse of this glorious scene, take note of Acts 1:9.

Heart Response

Pursuing godliness is all about Jesus Christ, dear one. *He* is the mystery of godliness, the mystery once hidden but now revealed. As believers in Christ and as women after God's own heart, we have the ability—and the precious privilege!—to live lives of godliness. What a wonderful reality! What a wonderful possession to share with others! Oh, may we never let the passing of time crowd out this wonderful message of the awesome mystery of Christ in us, the hope of glory! As a woman pursuing godliness, don't lose sight of the truth of the gospel of Jesus Christ, as this story so tragically describes.

There once was an old church in England. A sign on the front of the building read, "We preach Christ crucified." After a time, ivy grew up and obscured the last word. The motto now read, "We preach Christ." The ivy grew some more, and the motto read, "We preach." Finally, ivy covered the entire sign, and the church died. Such is the fate of any church that fails to carry out its mission in the world.[19]

Lesson 11

Identifying False Teachers

1 Timothy 4:1-5

*I*t's been said that "repetition is the mother of all skill." In the case of Paul's message today, repetition is vital for developing the well-honed skill of identifying false teaching and false teachers! Paul, the ever-concerned shepherd and watchman, takes great care to warn...and warn...and warn again...and again...about the danger of deception to believers in Christ Jesus. Note the number of times the passionate Paul brings up this subject:

1. Paul's concern for false teachers was first expressed to the Ephesian elders when Paul met them on his way to Jerusalem (Acts 20:29-30).

2. Some four years later, as we've already read in lesson 2, Paul wrote to warn Timothy about watching out for false teachers (1 Timothy 1:3-11).

3. Paul's growing concern for the possibility of apostasy now prompts him to pen yet another warning (1 Timothy 4:1-5).

4. And, for your information, Paul isn't finished watching and warning...as we'll see in lesson 20 (1 Timothy 6:3-5)!

Don't you think, in light of the emphasis Paul places on this problem in the church, that we should pay double attention as Paul, through the distinct prompting of the Holy Spirit, sounds the alarm a second time? May we take heed to Paul's many warnings!

1 Timothy 4:1-5

¹ Now the Spirit expressly says that in latter times some will depart from the faith, giving heed to deceiving spirits and doctrines of demons,

² speaking lies in hypocrisy, having their own conscience seared with a hot iron,

³ forbidding to marry, and commanding to abstain from foods which God created to be received with thanksgiving by those who believe and know the truth.

⁴ For every creature of God is good, and nothing is to be refused if it is received with thanksgiving;

⁵ for it is sanctified by the word of God and prayer.

Out of God's Word...

1. Comb through verses 1 and 2 and list how false teachers and their followers are identified.

2. Now note the erroneous teachings of false teachers in verse 3.

3. How does Paul say we are to receive God's good creation (verses 3-4)?

4. Why can we receive every good creation with thanksgiving (verses 4-5)?

...and into Your Heart

In the Old Testament, God placed certain restrictions on His people, especially with respect to food. These restrictions were to keep His chosen people, the Jews, separated and distinct from the heathen nations surrounding them. Later, however, God lifted the restrictions on foods.

• What did Jesus say about this lifting of food restrictions in Mark 7:15-19?

And what lesson did Jesus' disciple Peter learn concerning the eating of food in Acts 10:13-15?

• One tactic false teachers use is to try to go "one up" on God. For instance, God says salvation is by grace alone (Ephesians 2:8-9). But false teachers say one needs something more. In the case of marriage, God instituted marriage in Genesis 2:22-24. What did the false teachers in Paul and Timothy's day teach was a more (or "one up") spiritual view toward marriage (1 Timothy 4:3)?

And, as we learned above, Jesus declared all food clean in Mark 7. But what did the false teachers say was more spiritual (1 Timothy 4:3)?

- From what source did these false teachers derive their doctrine according to verse 1?

- Aren't you glad Paul's text ends on a positive note (verse 5)?! What do these Scriptures say about an attitude of thankfulness?

  Ephesians 5:20—

  Colossians 3:17—

  1 Thessalonians 5:18—

*W*hat a pity is it that this earth, which is so full of God's goodness, should be empty of his praises....[20]

List here at least five things you are thankful for. Be sure you are not among "the multitudes that live upon God's bounty"[21] and fail to give thanks!

What can you do today to express your thankfulness to God and to others?

- Paul states that food is sanctified by the word of God and prayer (1 Timothy 4:5). As we noted above, Jesus Himself (Mark 7) and Peter's instruction from God (Acts 10) became the standard for New Testament believers. These revelations in the Word of God, along with thankful prayers, make it possible for Christians to eat any food with a clear conscience (with one exception—see 1 Corinthians 8:13).

I like the beauty of one researcher's thoughts on the issue of food and God's cleansing of it...and our gratitude for it:

> *As* we recognize God's hand in all the pleasures of his creation and as we offer him thanks, we take what is ordinary and make it extraordinary. In short, we sanctify it, or "set it apart for special use," by making it a reason to praise and honor God.[22]

Heart Response

Godliness, dear one, is not achieved by adding or subtracting from God's Word. True godliness manifests itself in a thankful and prayerful attitude. Why not take a few moments right now and thank God for His abundant provision for you and your family? And for the simplicity of your salvation.

Lesson 12

Exercising Yourself
in Godliness

1 Timothy 4:6-16

ver the years, my husband has watched his share of football games (as I told you earlier). And I generally try to sit with Jim when it's game time (...always with a few of my personal projects nearby to work on). I admit to pretending to be interested—except when our college team is playing. Anyway, in trying to explain what's happening, Jim will often say, "The best defense is a good offense." (Or is it, "The best offense is a good defense"?)

Well, I may be confused, but when it came to the apostle Paul and the battle for the truth in the church, *he* most definitely knew what was going on! And in this lesson he's proposing that the best way for his young disciple, Timothy, to defend against error is for him to faithfully discharge his duties as a good minister and to conduct himself properly before the Ephesian church. This "offensive measure" would then counter the behavior of the false teachers. Let's look at the advice the wise older apostle, Paul, gives to the younger pastor, Timothy.

1 Timothy 4:6-16

6 If you instruct the brethren in these things, you will be a good minister of Jesus Christ, nourished in the words of faith and of the good doctrine which you have carefully followed.

7 But reject profane and old wives' fables, and exercise yourself rather to godliness.

8 For bodily exercise profits a little, but godliness is profitable for all things, having promise of the life that now is and of that which is to come.

9 This is a faithful saying and worthy of all acceptance.

10 For to this end we both labor and suffer reproach, because we trust in the living God, who is the Savior of all men, especially of those who believe.

11 These things command and teach.

12 Let no one despise your youth, but be an example to the believers in word, in conduct, in love, in spirit, in faith, in purity.

13 Till I come, give attention to reading, to exhortation, to doctrine.

14 Do not neglect the gift that is in you, which was given to you by prophecy with the laying on of the hands of the presbytery.

15 Meditate on these things; give yourself entirely to them, that your progress may be evident to all.

16 Take heed to yourself and to the doctrine. Continue in them, for in doing this you will save both yourself and those who hear you.

Out of God's Word...

Having just described the apostasy that was coming (1 Timothy 4:1—see lesson 11), Paul now gives Timothy advice on how to strengthen both himself and the church under his care against the error to come. Now, in this lesson, which divides into two sections, Paul tells Timothy how he can be seen as a "good minister of Jesus Christ."

1. *Pastoral instructions*—First Paul gives Timothy guidance on being a "good minister." List several of Paul's pastoral instructions (verses 6-11).

   How did Paul contrast bodily exercise with godliness in verses 7 and 8?

2. *Personal instructions*—Next Paul gives advice to Timothy about his personal conduct. List several of Paul's personal instructions (verses 12-16).

   What is the ultimate result of a godly ministry (verse 16)?

...and into Your Heart

- Are you wondering why this Bible study is titled *Pursuing Godliness?* Well, dear friend, the word *godliness* occurs eight times in the book of 1 Timothy. So far we've encountered *godliness* in 1 Timothy 2:2,10 and 3:16. And now here in 1 Timothy 4:7 and 8 we again meet up with our recurring theme of "pursuing godliness." Once again, what did Paul say about pursuing godliness in...

...verse 7?

...verse 8?

• Instead of occupying himself with fruitless activities and "fables," Timothy is urged to keep on disciplining himself toward godliness, to keep on seeking to please God in all his activities. In other words, he is to "labor" to the point of exhaustion (verse 10) in his quest of godliness. What are your thoughts concerning the concept of exercising your spiritual life in the same way you would exercise your physical body? And why do you think Paul thought it was important?

What are some things you can do to develop a better "exercise schedule" for your spiritual life? Make note of at least three and then read the following challenge to exercise yourself in godliness.

*K*eeping the body with all of its desires and passions under discipline is worth something, is in fact a part of a true life of godliness. But it is only a small part, for true godliness has its seat in the spirit, not in bodily discipline. Godliness is not achieved through a rigorous mortification of the body in order to control the spirit, it is rather the spiritual in control of the body.[23]

- One more important statement made by Paul was about "the Savior of all men" (verse 10). Paul cannot be teaching that all men will be saved in a spiritual sense. The Bible clearly teaches that God will not save everyone. This is a good way to explain this verse: "In this life, all men experience to some degree the protecting, delivering, sustaining power of God. Believers will experience that to the fullest degree for time and for all eternity."[24]

Heart Response

Paul advises Timothy to consider *his* conduct and to exercise *him*self in godliness in several ways. And I thought that a good heart "exercise" for *us* as women after God's own heart would be to evaluate *our*selves along with Timothy in these areas:

Are you a godly example...

in word (speech)

in conduct

in love (for both God and man)

in spirit

in faith (faithfulness)

in purity

Are you giving attention...

to reading (God's Word)

to exhorting (God's people)

to doctrine (God's truth)

to development (God's gifts)

Now, as Paul said, give yourself entirely to these things!

Lesson 13

Caring for Others

1 Timothy 5:1-2

One Sunday, as Jim and I sat in church looking at the bulletin that had been placed in our hands by the greeter at the door, we noticed the following announcement set off in a little box:

> *Biblical Counseling 101* will be offered as an adult elective. This is an in-depth discipleship class that will help you in your own walk with the Lord, so that you in turn can help others. If you are interested in attending, you must sign up with the Pastor by November 19th.

Today's lesson might well be called "Biblical Counseling 101." Paul is telling Timothy exactly how to approach the different groups in the church. Paul is letting him know exactly how to speak to others in the body of Christ when they are in sin and need to be exhorted.

So let's sit in on Paul's inspired class on biblical counseling.

1 Timothy 5:1-2

¹ Do not rebuke an older man, but exhort him as a father, the younger men as brothers,

² the older women as mothers, the younger as sisters, with all purity.

Out of God's Word...

1. Before we learn about how Timothy was to help others with *their* conduct, read again 1 Timothy 4:6-16 and note how Timothy was to conduct *himself*. Note two or three points of Paul's instruction that stood out to you.

2. Here in 1 Timothy 5:1-2, Paul divides the church congregation into four groups. What are they?

   _____   _____

   _____   _____

3. Next Paul gives specific advice for counseling or confronting each group. How was each group to be treated?

   Older men—(verse 1)?

Younger men—(verse 1)?

Older women—(verse 2)?

Younger women—(verse 2)?

What further caution does Paul give Timothy concerning his dealings with the younger women (verse 2)?

...and into Your Heart

- In his instructions to Timothy, Paul mentioned two approaches for counseling and confronting the various kinds of church members. The first is *rebuke*. The word for rebuke used here literally means to strike or beat with a blow, and metaphorically means to pound with words or to reprimand. Paul says "strike not hard upon" or rebuke not sharply those in the "family of God" who have sinned.

  As you think about how you handle people, do you recognize any tendency to strike harshly or scold with words?

  If you're a mom, how do you handle the "little people" in your home?

  How does Paul's *Biblical Counseling 101* show you a better way?

- The second approach for counseling is *exhortation*. Exhort means to come alongside someone in order to help them, with the intention and purpose of strengthening them.

What does Paul tell us about our role in restoring a sinning Christian in Galatians 6:1-2?

In 1 Thessalonians 5:14, Paul gives us even more advice on biblical counseling. What does he teach there about how to handle different groups of people and their problems?

How does Paul's *Biblical Counseling 101* show you a better way of assisting others with their problems?

* Just one more word of advice: Respectful treatment of the opposite sex will preserve purity (verse 2). When our attitude and actions toward opposite-gender members of the church are based on godly motives (i.e., strengthening, encouraging, helping, and comforting), then suspicion of impropriety will be greatly eliminated.

As a woman pursuing godliness, what can you do to be certain that your dealings in the church with the opposite sex are above suspicion and with all purity?

Heart Response

And now for you and me, my friend. Our attitude toward the people in the church is to be that of a caring, loving family member toward another family member…even when they sin and err. Yes, we are to hate their sin, but, dear one, we are to love the sinner!

And don't you agree that a loving heart attitude is at the core of caring for others? Isn't the way we treat others based on our heart attitude toward others? Jesus, the Ultimate Biblical Counselor, said, "Out of the abundance of the heart the mouth speaks" (Matthew 12:34). It's true that we speak and act out of what is in our hearts.

So how about a heart checkup? How's *your* heart when it comes to caring for others? Do you...

—Love one another (John 13:34-35)?

—Pray for one another (Ephesians 6:18)?

—Respect one another (Philippians 2:3-4)?

—Comfort one another (1 Thessalonians 5:11)?

—Edify one another (1 Thessalonians 5:11)?

esson 14

Caring for Widows

he thought of becoming a widow is not pleasant, is it? But, according to any life insurance agent's statistics, most of us who are married will outlive our husbands. (In fact, widows outnumber widowers four to one.) Fortunately, due to our present stable economy here in America, most widows will have some measure of financial provision for their future—their husband's life insurance, savings and retirement accounts, their personal social security, etc. And even if there are no funds available, God promises He will see to it that His widows are taken care of (Psalm 68:5; Proverbs 15:25; James 1:27).

But in A.D. 63, when young Timothy was pastoring the church at Ephesus, widows did not have the insurance protection or retirement provisions we enjoy today. With no ability to work outside the home and no means to support themselves, widows were completely at the mercy of others.

Apparently the care of widows was becoming a major burden for the Ephesian church. So Paul now begins his instruction on *who* should take care of *which* widows. Believe me, something is here for *every* woman!

1 Timothy 5:3-8

3 Honor widows who are really widows.

4 But if any widow has children or grandchildren, let them first learn to show piety at home and to repay their parents; for this is good and acceptable before God.

5 Now she who is really a widow, and left alone, trusts in God and continues in supplications and prayers night and day.

6 But she who lives in pleasure is dead while she lives.

7 And these things command, that they may be blameless.

8 But if anyone does not provide for his own, and especially for those of his household, he has denied the faith and is worse than an unbeliever.

Out of God's Word...

1. Here in 1 Timothy 5, Paul begins his instructions about caring for widows with a command to Timothy and the church. What is that command (verse 3)?

Next Paul identifies two classes of widows. What are they (verses 4 and 5)?

Family members were to be the primary and natural providers for their widowed relatives. What does Paul have to say on this subject (verse 4)?

And what duty was the church to have toward those widows who had no family (verses 3 and 16)?

2. Describe the widow that Paul considered to be a *true* widow (verse 5).

3. What comments did Paul have regarding family members who *did* care for their widowed parents (verse 4)?

And how did Paul view family members who did *not* take care of their widowed parents (verse 8)?

...and into Your Heart

- *The widows*—Paul has a lot to say about widows. (In fact, this passage—which we are taking three lessons to cover—is 14 verses long!) What beautiful spiritual portrait does Paul paint of the true widow in verse 5?

  Now look at the beautiful portrait of Anna in Luke 2:36-38. What similarities do you see in her that Paul describes here in 1 Timothy 5?

- *The families*—Paul also has a lot to say about the families of widows. What was one of God's Ten Commandments to children in Exodus 20:12?

And what did Paul write to the Ephesians on this same theme in Ephesians 6:1-2?

*T*o the Greek poet Euriphedes, the most haunting sin ever was failure in one's duty to a parent.

What scathing summation does Paul have for children who neglect to care for their widowed parents and grandparents (1 Timothy 5:8)?

On the other hand, how is true godliness, or *piety,* shown to our relatives, and how is it viewed by God (verse 4)?

In what ways are you currently looking out for the welfare of your parents, grandparents, and in-laws?

In what ways are you planning to look out for the welfare of your parents, grandparents, and in-laws in the future?

- *The church*—Earlier when we studied the institution of the office of deacon, we looked at Acts 6:1-4. Read that account again and describe the issue with the widows in the early church.

How was the problem resolved?

How does *your church* presently minister to the needs of its widows?

How are *you* currently ministering to the needs of the widows in your church? What means do you have at your disposal to assist them?

Heart Response

Well, it's heart-to-heart time. And this is *truly* from my heart to yours! I remember telling a group of women that my husband and I don't even pray about taking care of our parents—it's a "given" in Scripture and not something we need to pray about. We just do it, we have just done it, and we will just keeping on doing it. Well, I have to tell you that *I* was shocked when I noticed the shock on *their* faces at such a statement! And, believe me, there was quite a discussion afterwards!

But here it is, my friend—right here in 1 Timothy 5! Knowing what Paul said here in the book of 1 Timothy moved Jim to make such a decision regarding our own families long ago. And I have to say, after caring for Jim's mother (who was widowed twice) until she died, we have no regrets. The same applies to my father, whom we assisted until his death at 96. And now we are assisting with the care for my own widowed mother.

This Bible study series is titled "A Woman After God's Own Heart." I want to be a woman after God's own heart, and I know you do, too. And, beloved, this is one thing that a woman after God's own heart does—she cares for her family members. Yes, it takes time. And it takes money and effort. And...it is good and acceptable in the sight of *God!*

Lesson 15

Giving to Others

1 Timothy 5:9-10

How can a woman know, beyond a shadow of a doubt, that her life has counted? Today's lesson gives us a checklist for godly character and a life of good works. Let's hurry on and find out what the Lord's standards are for those like you and me who yearn to lead a lovely and useful life.

(And P.S.—Don't forget to notice that such godly character and good works are being produced in the painful crucible of bereavement.)

1 Timothy 5:9-10

⁹ Do not let a widow under sixty years old be taken into the number, and not unless she has been the wife of one man,

¹⁰ well reported for good works: if she has brought up children, if she has lodged strangers, if she has washed the saints' feet, if she has relieved the afflicted, if she has diligently followed every good work.

Out of God's Word...

1. Now that Paul has addressed the issue of caring for widows, he turns his attention to the qualifications of those widows the church will care for. First of all, what is the *age* requirement (verse 9)?

   And what is the *marital* requirement (verse 9)?

   Next Paul addresses the *personal* requirements (verse 10). Paul notes first an overarching qualification of reputation and then five specific works. List all six here.

   _____   _____

   _____   _____

   _____   _____

...and into Your Heart

- First, a few words of explanation that will help our understanding

  "Taken into the number" refers to an official church list of widows who were supported by the church.

"The wife of one man" most likely does not mean that a widow who had remarried after her first husband's death was disapproved from being supported by the church (see 1 Timothy 5:14). Rather it means that *while* the widow was married, she was faithful to her husband.

- Now let's look at how the widow whom Paul is describing spent her life giving to others.

  —"Well reported for good works." As we noted earlier, this is an all-encompassing statement about a godly widow's reputation. How was godliness defined in 1 Timothy 2:10?

  When others think of *you*, dear one, would they describe *you* as a woman of good works and noble deeds? Explain why or why not and what you can do about becoming a woman of good works.

  —"If she has brought up children." This "good work" of the godly widow could refer to either bringing up her own children and grandchildren or to orphaned children. As one Bible commentator so eloquently explains, "here her godliness and moral standards are readily displayed. To rear children well is worthy of highest praise."[25] If you're a mom, do you consider raising your children to follow the Lord as a "good work"—indeed one of your *highest* and *greatest* works (see again 1 Timothy 2:15)? If not, what adjustment must you make in your perception of this privileged role and responsibility?

  —"If she has lodged strangers." This is another way of saying that this woman practiced hospitality. Keep in mind that there were no Motel 6 or Holiday Inn chains in Paul's day! Christians away from home depended upon women, like the one Paul is describing, for food and a safe place to stay. Is this shining grace true of you?

—"If she has washed the saints' feet." This expression was most likely literal, referring to the Oriental custom of washing the dirty feet of guests as they entered the house. It exemplifies humble service. Jesus humbled Himself to wash the feet of His disciples (John 13:14). Can you think of some ways you, too, exhibit or could exhibit humble service to others?

—"If she has relieved the afflicted." Keep in mind, too, that Christians in the early church were persecuted and oppressed! They needed relief and help...and dear women like this one delighted in rendering such ministry. Who do you know who needs relief and help?

—"If she has diligently followed every good work." In other words, this noble woman was devoted to every kind of good work! Pursuing godliness means pursuing good deeds. Is such a godly goal on the top of your daily to-do list?

Heart Response

What a rich passage! I could go on and on in praise of these verses and what they have meant to me as a woman. It's what I call one of "the pink passages" of the Bible, one of the sections in God's Word that spells out for you and me as women after God's own heart exactly what it means to be a true woman of excellence. Verse 10 especially shows us God's priorities and God's standard and God's design for our everyday lives. In short, God calls us to a life of good works.

Perhaps because Christmas has just passed (it's January 2 as I write this), this little poem about giving to others seemed most appropriate for summing up the goodness in a life of service to others. As I read it, I couldn't help but think of the many needy people down through the centuries who have been blessed by the selfless giving of saints like the widow Paul describes for us in verse 10. May you and I, dear one, join her worthy rank!

> Somehow, not only for Christmas
> But all the year long through,
> The joy that you give to others
> Is the joy that comes back to you.
>
> And the more you spend in blessing
> The poor and the lonely and sad,
> The more of your heart's possessions
> Return to make you glad.[26]

Lesson 16

Living Above Reproach

1 Timothy 5:11-16

The story of *Beauty and the Beast* has been around for a long time. But maybe, after reading today's lesson, you'll agree with me that it's obviously been around a lot longer than we thought! **Warning:** What you are about to read contains words and behaviors that may be offensive! (And I hope they are!)

Now, we met up with *beauty* in our previous lesson. Brace yourself for the *beast!*

1 Timothy 5:11-16

¹¹ But refuse the younger widows; for when they have begun to grow wanton against Christ, they desire to marry,

¹² having condemnation because they have cast off their first faith.

¹³ And besides they learn to be idle, wandering about from house to house, and not only idle but also gossips and busybodies, saying things which they ought not.

¹⁴ Therefore I desire that the younger widows marry, bear children, manage the house, give no opportunity to the adversary to speak reproachfully.

¹⁵ For some have already turned aside after Satan.

¹⁶ If any believing man or woman has widows, let them relieve them, and do not let the church be burdened, that it may relieve those who are really widows.

Out of God's Word...

1. We've heard Paul on the issue of widows in the church (lesson 14) and on the older widows in the church (lesson 15). Now he turns his attention to the younger widows. What advice does Paul give regarding the younger widows in verse 11 and why?

2. What were some other problems with the younger widows (verse 13)?

3. What additional comment does Paul make concerning some of these younger widows (verse 15)?

4. Having stated the problems this group of widows faced, what advice does Paul give to the church leaders and why (verse 14)?

5. Once again, what instructions to all does Paul repeat (see verse 4) in verse 16?

...and into Your Heart

- Just as we did in our previous lesson, let's consider a few things that will help us with our understanding of what it means to live above reproach.

  "When they have begun to grow wanton against Christ, they desire to marry" (verse 11). Sensual desires can sometimes lead a woman to rebel and marry an unbeliever.

  "They have cast off their first faith" (verse 12). One scholar explains these words in this way: "They become pagans again to suit a pagan husband, thus their 'first faith' is rejected, thrown aside, for a second (false) faith."[27]

  "Give no opportunity to the adversary to speak reproachfully" (verse 14). Any human adversary of Christianity would be quick to use any scandal to revile the name of Jesus and discredit the gospel.

  "Some have already turned aside after Satan" (verse 15). As my pastor explains this, "Some of the younger widows had abandoned their vows to Christ....They were no longer serving Christ, but Satan."[28]

- If nothing else, I hope you are beginning to acknowledge the seriousness of the problems these younger widows faced and were, in some cases, succumbing to. Now for some application! Consider these three principles:

  Being self-controlled—Any woman, married or single or widowed, can give in to sensuality and dishonor the name of Christ. First note the list of what Paul calls "the works of the flesh" in Galatians 5:19-21. Which ones of these "works" describes the "wantonness" Paul refers to in 1 Timothy 5:11? And what provision has God made for believers, according to Galatians 5:22-23?

Are there any curbs you need to put on your own desires?

(And, by the way, what does the Bible say about marrying unbelievers in 2 Corinthians 6:14-15?)

Behavior—In verse 13 Paul gives us a pretty awful list of behaviors that *many* women exhibit! These, dear one, are bad habits produced by idleness. And gadding about from house to house doesn't generally breed good habits either! These women were making the rounds and instead of being busy *workers* for the cause of Christ they were busy*bodies!* Are any of their behaviors true of your life too? Be specific...and be ruthless! As I said above, this is *very* serious business! Now, what "ruthless" or radical steps can you take to ensure that your behavior is above reproach and matches the standard set by the woman in verse 10?

Benefits of marriage—Paul, under the inspiration of the Holy Spirit, states that these idle widows should get married! His view is that a husband to care for, children to raise, and a house to keep will definitely better their behavior and contribute positively to the church, to the community, and to the name of Christ. What does Titus 2:3-5 have to say about marriage, family, and homelife? Do you hold these same views? Why or why not?

Heart Response

As I read through this lesson and the Bible text, the sweet aroma of the other, older group of widows was still lingering around my desk. And I couldn't help but compare the beauty of the "good works" of those dear older widows with the scandalous, destructive "works" of this on-the-go younger group—the beasts! What wasted time...and energy...and lives! What missed opportunities to do something *useful,* to better the lives of *others,* to do something constructive and of *eternal value!*

So I want to leave us with a checklist for character drawn from 1 Timothy 5:9-10—from the *good* widows and from their *good* works. It applies to every woman after God's own heart, married or single or widowed, young or old. Oh, please, may your life and mine be one of good works!

- ✓ *Overall conduct*—Good words are spoken of a woman of good works. She earns her good reputation by living above reproach and doing good deeds of all kinds. Good deeds like these...

- ✓ *Hospitality to strangers*—Using your home and hearth to welcome traveling Christians and to entertain fellow believers is a good way to put your time and energy to work.

- ✓ *Help for those in trouble*—Using your strength to assist those who suffer is a hands-on ministry that gives glory to God.

- ✓ *Washing the feet of the saints*—Compassion and benevolence and perhaps, more specifically, visits to the needy, the ill, the shut-in are a good use of time and bring basic benefits to those you serve.

- ✓ *Devotion to every good work*—Devote yourself—time, energy, efforts, and heart—diligently to pursuing a life of good works.[29]

Lesson 17

Honoring Leaders

1 Timothy 5:17-18

I've often heard it said that a church rises or falls on the spiritual maturity of its leadership. And I recently had this saying affirmed as I sat with my husband and our daughter Courtney and her husband in a New Year's Eve praise service at their church. Person after person gave praise for the increased church attendance and new members. And, amazingly, person after person gave praise for godly leaders, mature leaders. It seemed that the two praiseworthy items—godly leadership and church growth—went hand in hand!

Paul certainly recognized the significance of a strong, vibrant, and growing leadership (as we've already seen many times in this first letter to Timothy). His epistle is about pursuing godliness, and it's interesting to note that the groups that have received the most attention concerning their godly character are the leaders—the elders, deacons, and deaconesses.

Today we learn that Paul believes such leaders should be honored for their diligence, commitment, and godliness. Hear now what he recommends for the "worthy" leader.

1 Timothy 5:17-18

[17] Let the elders who rule well be counted worthy of double honor, especially those who labor in the word and doctrine.

[18] For the Scripture says, "You shall not muzzle an ox while it treads out the grain," and, "The laborer is worthy of his wages."

Out of God's Word...

1. According to verse 17, what are three responsibilities of an elder?

2. What recognition should they receive (verse 17)?

3. And what authority does Paul quote to justify the elders being rewarded for their labors (verse 18)?

...and into Your Heart

- *The office*—Look again at 1 Timothy 3:1-7. What term was used for these men who are here (5:17) called elders?

  And briefly, what qualified them for the office of elder (1 Timothy 3:1-7)?

  Now read Titus 1:5-9 and note additional and similar qualifications.

- *The honor*—Paul tells Timothy (and us) to honor our church leaders. What do these additional Scriptures say about our attitude and behavior toward our leaders?

     1 Thessalonians 5:12-13—

     Hebrews 13:7 and 17—

  For your information...double honor points to the honor which comes to an elder because of his *office* and that which he *obtains* by fulfilling his office well.

  Which particular elders did Paul especially want to receive double honor (verse 17)?

Double honor refers to an increase in respect and in appreciation. How can you show "double honor" to those who labor among you as leaders in your church...

...in respect?

...in appreciation?

• *The reward*—In verse 18 Paul refers to the Old Testament law in Deuteronomy 25:4 to support paying ministers. What was the principle presented in the Deuteronomy verse?

Paul also quotes Jesus' words in Luke 10:7. What did Jesus say?

What role do you play in ensuring that the worthy ministers in your church receive the monetary reward that the Bible recommends?

Heart Response

How much is it worth to you and your family to have a godly minister and godly leadership in your church? No price tag can be put on men who faithfully lead, preach, and teach God's Word! I'm sure you've heard about or been involved in churches where the leadership was not faithful to the standards Paul sets up in his letter to Timothy. Why not purpose, along with me, to do three things. Let's...

—First, thank the Lord for our faithful leaders.

—Second, commit to show our appreciation, both monetarily and verbally, to the men in our church who are worthy of "double honor."

—Third, cease to criticize our leadership, as this gentleman suggests:

Care...or Criticism?

*F*aithful church leaders should be supported and appreciated. Too often they are targets for criticism because the congregation has unrealistic expectations. How do you treat your church leaders? Do you enjoy finding fault, or do you show your appreciation? Do they receive enough financial support to allow them to live without worry and to provide for the needs of their families? Unfortunately, we often take church leaders for granted by not providing adequately for their needs or by subjecting them to heavy criticism. Think of ways you can "honor" your preachers and teachers.[30]

Examining Leaders

1 Timothy 5:19-25

good reputations is hard to come by. It's been said that a good reputation takes a lifetime to develop but can be lost in a moment.

Let's listen in as the apostle Paul outlines a plan for protecting the church and protecting the good reputation of its leaders. Paul bases his "plan" on Deuteronomy 19:15-19, a portion of the Old Testament law which deals with protection from false witness.

1 Timothy 5: 19-25

[19] Do not receive an accusation against an elder except from two or three witnesses.

²⁰ Those who are sinning rebuke in the presence of all, that the rest also may fear.

²¹ I charge you before God and the Lord Jesus Christ and the elect angels that you observe these things without prejudice, doing nothing with partiality.

²² Do not lay hands on anyone hastily, nor share in other people's sins; keep yourself pure.

²³ No longer drink only water, but use a little wine for your stomach's sake and your frequent infirmities.

²⁴ Some men's sins are clearly evident, preceding them to judgment, but those of some men follow later.

²⁵ Likewise, the good works of some are clearly evident, and those that are otherwise cannot be hidden.

Out of God's Word...

1. What caution is given on receiving an accusation against an elder (verse 19)?

   And what must happen if the accusation is confirmed (verse 20)?

   And what was pastor Timothy's role in the process of examining elders (verse 21)?

2. Perhaps to keep the above problem from occurring, Paul gives advice to Timothy about selecting leaders. What caution does Paul impart in verse 22?

3. Note Paul's two observations concerning examining the lives of potential elders for *sin* (verse 24).

Observation #1—

Observation #2—

4. Now note Paul's two observations concerning examining the lives of potential elders for *good works* (verse 25).

Observation #1—

Observation #2—

5. In addition to instruction on examining elders, what bits of fatherly advice does Paul have for his "son" Timothy (verses 22 and 23)?

...and into Your Heart

Obviously this is a heart-to-heart talk between Paul and Timothy regarding high-level management and leadership principles for the church. Paul is explaining to young pastor Timothy the ins and outs of his role, and examining leaders was an important part of that role...and it was serious business!

Two principles stand out in this passage—two principles that speak clearly to every Christian who is pursuing godliness—leader or nonleader, whether elder or church member. So let's examine ourselves by the principles. Surely before we have any part in evaluating leaders...or anyone else...we must take care to examine ourselves first!

• *Principle #1*—Sin cannot be hidden. Paul says sin will be evident...sooner or later (verse 24). What does Moses say in Numbers 32:23 about this principle?

Sin is a fact, a reality. What does 1 John 1:8 tell us about our sin?

Rather than denying sin, we should be searching for it. What was the gist of David's heartfelt prayer in Psalm 139:23-24?

What solution does Proverbs 28:13 offer to the problem of sin?

As you examine *your* heart, do you uncover any area of sin that you need to confess and forsake? What are your plans to do so? (And don't forget to ask for God's gracious help—1 John 1:9.)

• *Principle #2*—Good works cannot be hidden. Just as sin is either evident or will become exposed, so good works are either evident or will come to light (1 Timothy 5:25). What does Proverbs 27:2 say about this principle?

Most people want their good works to be noticed. (Indeed, some do good works for that express purpose—Matthew 6:1-2!) But what did Jesus have to say about our good works in Matthew 6:6?

For your information...the good work of Queen Esther's cousin, Mordecai, went unnoticed and unrewarded for five years (Esther 6:1-3)! Could you go that long...or longer...without being noticed for your good deeds?

Heart Response

Do you feel like you're eavesdropping as you read and work your way through this passage, my friend? Does it seem like you're a visitor at a father/son talk? At a high-level meeting? I do. Timothy is a pastor, and Paul is a man's man, a teacher's teacher, a leader's leader. And he's giving straight-forward direction to his young protégé.

Well, dear one, the Bible gives you and me straight-forward direction, too, about our conduct in the church. Here are a few do's and don'ts to take to heart.

Do examine your own life.

Do pursue godliness.

Do pray for purity in your leadership.

Do trust God with the lives and actions of others.

Don't be a part of causing trouble in the church (Philippians 4:1-2).

Don't be a part of gossiping and tearing down the hard-won reputations of others (1 Timothy 3:11; Titus 2:3).

Lesson 19

Serving in the Workplace

1 Timothy 6:1-2

imothy was a very blessed man! When I reflect on his relationship with Paul, his mentor, I can only wish the same for everyone! Just think about it—five chapters (so far), filled with doctrinal teaching, practical pointers, and insights into dealing with tough church-related issues. This letter from Paul to Timothy is truly loaded with the how-to's and the ins-and-outs of pastoring a church.

And Paul isn't finished yet! Today's lesson addresses another issue of Paul and Timothy's day—the proper behavior of slaves who were becoming Christians.

It is estimated that in Paul's day one half of the world's population—or 60 million people!—were slaves. The message of salvation and freedom in Christ appealed to slaves, and many of them became believers...which led to a new problem: Some of the slaves began to use their newfound freedom in Christ as an excuse to disobey and even defy their masters.

So here comes Paul with instructions for Timothy that must be passed on to those in his congregation who were slaves...about how to serve in the workplace and respond to their masters in the right way—God's way.

1 Timothy 6:1-2

¹ Let as many servants as are under the yoke count their own masters worthy of all honor, so that the name of God and His doctrine may not be blasphemed.

² And those who have believing masters, let them not despise them because they are brethren, but rather serve them because those who are benefited are believers and beloved. Teach and exhort these things.

Out of God's Word...

1. To begin, what command did Paul give to Timothy at the end of verse 2?

2. How are servants or slaves to treat their masters, according to verse 1?

What reason was given for this attitude (verse 1)?

(And just as a special "womanly" exercise, what does Titus 2:5 tell us as wives?)

3. In the case of a believing slave who served a believing master, what instruction was given and why (verse 2)?

Instead, the slave in this situation was to _____ his Christian master for what two reasons?

   #1—

   #2—

4. For your information...the word *honor* in verse 1 is the same as showing *honor* to widows (1 Timothy 5:3) and double *honor* to elders (1 Timothy 5:17).

...and into Your Heart

• Paul's counsel addresses the master/slave relationship, an important issue in his day. In fact, he had already given the Ephesian church his directives on this matter (Ephesians 6:5-9). The principles of the master/slave relationship also apply, in the broad sense, to our twenty-first century workplace. "Masters" and "slaves" now become employers and employees. What did Paul and others have to say about both masters and slaves (or employers and employees)?

   Ephesians 6:5-9—

   Colossians 3:22–4:1—

   Titus 2:9-10—

   1 Peter 2:18—

In your own words, what was the attitude of a slave to be to his or her master and a master to be to his or her slave?

• What do these Scriptures teach about godly attitudes toward work?

   1 Corinthians 10:31—

   Colossians 3:17,23—

   1 Thessalonians 4:11-12—

• And in another category, how was the church to treat those who would not work (2 Thessalonians 3:10)?

• A Christian's proper attitude about work will affect how people view God and the message of salvation. So, if these categories apply to you...how would others rate you...

   ...as an employer?

   ...as an employee?

Heart Response

Work, whether in or out of the home, is important to God. Why? Because our attitude toward work is a reflection of our attitude toward God. God asks us to do our work heartily unto Him. He also asks that we serve our employers wholeheartedly and that we treat our employees fairly and with respect. Our obedience or disobedience to God's directives in the area of the workplace is easily seen by others.

Now for us, dear one. Are people getting an accurate picture of the reality of Jesus Christ from your life? If you and I are truly pursuing a life of godliness, then others will see the true gospel in our lives. As 2 Corinthians 3:2 reminds us, *we*—by our very lives—are living epistles, a Bible, known and read by all men.

So...what's the gospel according to you?

The Gospel According to You

The Gospels of Matthew, Mark, Luke and John,
Are read by more than a few,
But the one that is most read and commented on
Is the gospel according to *you*.

You are writing a gospel, a chapter each day
By things that you do and words that you say,
Men read what you write, whether faithless or true.
Say, what is the gospel according to *you*?

Do men read His truth and His love in your life,
Or has yours been too full of malice and strife?
Does your life speak of evil, or does it ring true?
Say, what is the gospel according to *you*?[31]

Recognizing False Teachers

*T*he Bible is an amazing book! It contains everything we need for life and godliness (2 Peter 1:3). God has packaged in this book a multitude of subjects. Yet, because the Bible is a book with an economy of words, when we see a teaching repeated again and again, we need to realize God wants us to pay close attention to what He is saying. Therefore, as students of the Bible, we should take special note if a subject is repeated.

Well, sit up and take note! Paul is now repeating—for the third time!—instructions concerning recognizing false teachers (see 1:3-11; 4:1-5; lessons 2 and 11). Obviously, God has a message for us!!

1 *Timothy 6:3-5*

³ If anyone teaches otherwise and does not consent to wholesome words, even the words of our Lord Jesus Christ, and to the doctrine which is according to godliness,

⁴ he is proud, knowing nothing, but is obsessed with disputes and arguments over words, from which come envy, strife, reviling, evil suspicions,

⁵ useless wranglings of men of corrupt minds and destitute of the truth, who suppose that godliness is a means of gain. From such withdraw yourself.

Out of God's Word...

1. Paul gives three warning signs for recognizing a false teacher. List them here from verse 3.

    He teaches _____.

    He does not consent to _____.

    He does not consent to _____.

    In addition, the false teacher is recognized by his personal flaws (verse 4).

    He is _____ and _____.

    He is _____.

2. Disputes and arguments over words lead to what five sins
   (verses 4 and 5)?

   _____   _____

   _____   _____

   _____

3. What are the final marks of a false teacher (verse 5)?

   _____ and _____

4. What erroneous assumption about "godliness" did the
   false teachers' corrupt thinking lead to (verse 5)?

5. And what is Paul's final instruction to his readers (verse 5)?

...and into Your Heart

From these three verses, let's pay special attention to three
telltale marks of a false teacher. Paul wanted Timothy to recognize these signs, and we can be sure he wanted the men
and women in the Ephesian church to recognize them. And
you and I need to recognize them, too.

• *Doctrine*—False teachers advocate a "different" doctrine,
  a teaching not committed to Scripture. They add to Scripture, take away from it, misinterpret it, or deny it altogether.[32] Beloved, their teaching did not agree with Paul's
  nor with the words of our Lord Jesus Christ.

Can you think of several ways *you* can grow in your knowledge of the Scripture so that you can better identify false teachers and false teaching?

- *Pride*—The arrogant teacher Paul describes is literally "wrapt in smoke" and filled with the fumes of self-conceit.[33] And in all his pride, he knows nothing—that is, nothing about the doctrine which is according to godliness.[34] "Pride" combines the idea of conceit and folly. The rejection of the evidence of the gospel is rooted in pride and is the utmost folly.[35]

  Pride has been at the root of most of mankind's problems. What do these verses teach us about pride?

  Proverbs 8:13—

  Proverbs 16:18—

  Also, what was one reason that a "novice" should not be selected as an elder (1 Timothy 3:6)?

  Are there areas where pride has crept into your life, my friend? Pride can affect any one of us and in a variety of ways…pride over wealth, possessions, education, knowledge, privilege, even pride about our humility! The list goes on and on. Be honest. And remember—pride comes before a fall.

- *Speech*—Words have a powerful effect. And the words of a false teacher bring forth the evil fruits of controversy instead of edification, strife instead of godliness, useless disputes, questions, theories, and fighting over words instead of truth. Have you ever tried to talk to a member of a cult about the truth of the gospel? Then you know exactly how such a conversation goes, and how frustrating it is (and also how frustrated you became!). That's what the "strife of words" leads to.

But you and I are called to *wholesome* words, healthy words, profitable words. What did Paul ask of the Ephesians (Ephesians 4:29)?

Beloved, Paul is asking the same thing of you and me in Ephesians 4:29. How are you doing? Do you make an effort to speak wholesome, gracious words of health and edification? Are there changes you need to make?

Heart Response

Do you yearn for a godly life, a holy life? Surely you do if you have made your way through 20 lessons of a study entitled *Pursuing Godliness*. One vital (and obvious) step in the pursuit of godliness is increasing in the knowledge of God's Word. God's Word will...

...provide the standard with which to recognize false teachers,

...protect you from false teaching, and

...produce godliness.

Hear the ultimate "word" on the Word of God—what it *is* and what it *does*—from Psalm 19:7-9.

The law of the LORD is perfect	converting the soul;
The testimony of the LORD is sure,	making wise the simple;
The statutes of the LORD are right,	rejoicing the heart;
The commandment of the LORD is pure,	enlightening the eyes;
The fear of the LORD is clean,	enduring forever;

The judgments of the LORD are true
and righteous altogether.

Now, my growing friend, what part does God's Word play in your plan for pursuing godliness?

Lesson 21

Loving Money

1 Timothy 6:6-10

I have to say that my model for life when it comes to godliness is the Proverbs 31 Woman. She has taught me well about the priorities of a godly life.

And the beautiful woman in Proverbs 31 also has a lot to say about money. She was truly a master manager of money! She was wise and she was thrifty. She earned money, saved money, invested money, managed money, spent money... and she gave money.

Beloved, there are many things that you and I can do in the money department, whether we have a job or not and whether we're married or not. We can shop wisely. We can clip coupons. We can manage our household on a budget.

We can even manage (sometimes, anyway!) to put a few coins aside for next Christmas or for home improvements. And, of course, we don't want to forget to give our money to others, just like the Proverbs 31 Woman did (Proverbs 31:20).

To add to our list of principles and precepts regarding money, Paul gets to the heart of the matter of money today and addresses "the love of money." Let's pay close attention so we can make sure we're on the right track as we pursue godliness, even in the area of money.

1 *Timothy 6:6-10*

6 But godliness with contentment is great gain.

7 For we brought nothing into this world, and it is certain we can carry nothing out.

8 And having food and clothing, with these we shall be content.

9 But those who desire to be rich fall into temptation and a snare, and into many foolish and harmful lusts which drown men in destruction and perdition.

10 For the love of money is a root of all kinds of evil, for which some have strayed from the faith in their greediness, and pierced themselves through with many sorrows.

Out of God's Word...

1. If you remember (and how could you forget!), in our last lesson we looked once again (for the third time!) at the marks of a false teacher. One mark is a warped attitude toward money and the ministry. What erroneous conclu-

sion does a false teacher come to regarding "godliness" and "gain" (or money) according to 1 Timothy 6:5?

For your information...the word "gain" means "worldliness," using the gospel as the means for becoming rich. It refers to money and income. See Titus 1:10-11 for an even clearer statement on the false teacher's motives.

2. Now Paul turns a corner and begins to let Timothy (and us) know what true godliness and "gain" is. What does verse 6 teach us will truly profit a Christian?

And why should we be content with what we have (verse 7)?

Paul boils contentment down to two necessities. What are they (verse 8)?

3. Describe the perils of riches (verse 9).

4. What aspect of money can lead to all sorts of evil (verse 10)?

And what happens to some who covet riches (verse 10)?

...and into Your Heart

Godliness. That's what we're pursuing in this entire study. And in 1 Timothy 6:6 we come across it again. As I think about this lesson on godliness and Paul's wisdom regarding money in 1 Timothy 6:6-10, it seems to fall into two categories.

• *Life*—Once again, what are the basics of life (verses 6-8)?

What was Job's perspective on life (Job 1:21)?

What was Paul's perspective on contentment and how it is realized (Philippians 4:11-13)?

Before you leave this truth and reality, take a look into your own heart, dear one. What do you see there when it comes to contentment? Are food and clothing enough? Do you spot any tendencies to desire more than is needed? As always, be specific.

Now be sure and take a moment and thank God for His abundant provision to you of the two necessities—food and clothing! I know I used this quotation earlier...but I didn't use all of it! So here it is in its entirety.

> *What* a pity it is that this earth, which is so full of God's goodness, should be empty of his praises, and that of the multitudes that live upon his bounty there are so few that live to his glory![36]

- *Lust*—Once again, how can lust and greed and worldliness and the desire for wealth corrupt us and lead us away from godliness and contentment (verses 9-10)?

What sin is inconsistent with contentment (Hebrews 13:5)?

What does 1 John 2:15-17 say about our affections toward the world?

Now take a few minutes to jot down some notes from these three examples of lust and discontentment.

Lot (Genesis 13:10-13)—

Achan (Judges 7:20-21)—

Satan (Isaiah 14:12-15)—

Also please notice that Paul did not say *money* is the root of all evil. He said *the love of money* is a root of all kinds of evil. Money is needed to buy food, clothing, and obtain shelter. We are to work for money in order to provide for the necessities of life (2 Thessalonians 3:10-12). The problem comes with a misplaced *desire* and a misplaced *affection*.

Before you leave this truth, take another look into your own heart. What do you see there when it comes to lust and greed? What can you do to check such desires? (Also don't forget to confess them as sin!)

Heart Response

I began this lesson by referring to the Proverbs 31 Woman, a truly godly woman (and a woman after God's own heart!) who has many wonderful lessons for you and me about life and management and priorities...and money. And now, dear one, I want to also end with her. Why? Because she also shows us a godly balance in this area of money.

First of all, her motives were pure—she desired to help and to better her family.

But second, her motives were godly—she gave her money to the poor and needy, assisting her community.

The best way to guard against the love of money is to be generous, dear godly sister. To be a "generous soul" (Proverbs 11:25). To have a "bountiful eye" (Proverbs 22:9). So…who needs your money today? What missionary's ministry could be bettered by a contribution from you? How could your church benefit from your liberality? Can you make a contribution to the poor and needy in your community? Ask God to assist you with this beautiful grace of giving (2 Corinthians 8:7). What a lovely way to pursue godliness!

esson 22

Fighting the
Good Fight of Faith

1 Timothy 6:11-16

idn't you enjoy studying the previous passage? It brought many wonderful messages to our hearts. But I especially liked leaving off with the pursuit of the beautiful grace of giving out of a gracious, generous heart in our quest for godliness.

However, in this lesson we come up against another side of pursuing godliness—a much more strenuous side—as Paul urges us to *fight*, to *struggle*, to *flee*, and to *pursue*. As you can already tell, this lesson will be full of effort, struggle, and action!

Perhaps you've had this same experience: you're looking for your favorite channel (in my case, that's The Weather

Channel!) or program on TV. So you begin flicking through the channels with your remote control. As image after image flashes by, you notice one of women...women in a wrestling ring...women brawling and body-slamming. It's not a very pretty sight!

Well, today Paul calls us to a wrestling match—to a fight to the finish. Unlike those phoney, glitzy Hollywood bouts I mentioned, we are to fight for something most worthy—the Christian faith. Let's allow Paul to explain.

1 Timothy 6:11-16

11 But you, O man of God, flee these things and pursue righteousness, godliness, faith, love, patience, gentleness.

12 Fight the good fight of faith, lay hold on eternal life, to which you were also called and have confessed the good confession in the presence of many witnesses.

13 I urge you in the sight of God who gives life to all things, and before Christ Jesus who witnessed the good confession before Pontius Pilate,

14 that you keep this commandment without spot, blameless until our Lord Jesus Christ's appearing,

15 which He will manifest in His own time, He who is the blessed and only Potentate, the King of kings and Lord of lords,

16 who alone has immortality, dwelling in unapproachable light, whom no man has seen or can see, to whom be honor and everlasting power. Amen.

Out of God's Word...

In this passage Paul is nearing the end of his letter to Timothy. Writing to Timothy in a very personal way, Paul gives his young friend and co-laborer a series of commands and a doxology.

Command #1: How does Paul refer to Timothy, and what is Paul's first command (verse 11)?

And what are "these things" according to verses 9 and 10?

Command #2: Now, moving on, Paul lists six better "things," godly things, to pursue. What are they (verse 11)?

_____   _____

_____   _____

_____   _____

Commands #3 and 4: Next Paul issues two more commands in verse 12. Note them now.

_____

_____

Command #5: Finally, what was Timothy asked to keep and for how long (verse 14)?

For your information, the commandment is "the entire truth of the Gospel which Timothy has confessed and which he has been commissioned to preach and to defend."[37]

Doxology: Paul breaks forth into a doxology of pure praise to God. Read it through reverently and note its many descriptions of the incomparable and inexpressible greatness of God (verses 15-16).

...*and into Your Heart*

- Timothy, a "man of God," was called by Paul to two actions: He was called to *flee* something and to *pursue* something. One action was negative and the other was positive. Negatively, he was to *flee* the love of money and its attendant evils. This is no mere turning of the back on these evils. No, it means to be ever fleeing, to never let them catch you, to realize that the margin of safety can never be too great.[38]

Positively, however, Timothy was to energetically *pursue* six godly virtues. As one explains...

> ...righteousness and godliness point to the attitude of the soul toward God.

> ...faith and love are the fountal source of the Christian life.

> ...patience and gentleness look outward and set forth the disposition necessary in those who encounter the antagonism of a Christ-rejecting world.[39]

Do words like *fleeing* and *energetic pursuit* describe your flight *away from* the love of money and *toward* the godly attitudes of the Christian life? What steps can you think of that would intensify the seriousness of these two actions in your daily life? Take care to record your thoughts here. This "heart response" is at the heart of pursuing godliness.

- As we are discovering, living the Christian life in all godliness demands strenuous effort. Next Paul called Timothy (and us) to *fight* the good fight of faith (verse 12). What strenuous efforts are you making in your "fight of faith"?

- How long must we fight? Paul answers that we should fight until our Lord Jesus Christ's appearing. We are better able to bear up in the battle when we look with eager anticipation to the Second Coming.

Does the struggle, the battle, of the Christian life ever cause you to look for and long for the return of your Lord? When was the last time you thought of the Lord's reappearance? (Or should I be asking, Do you *ever* think about the Lord's return?) Perhaps if we were fleeing from and following after and fighting hard enough, we might yearn more passionately for His return!

How much can you identify with the heart and words of this poem about the return of Jesus?

*J*esus, my Lord, Thou are coming!
  The signs are around us today.
Coming, dear Lord, Thou are coming;
  The times are preparing Thy way.

World-wide conditions portentous,
  Undreamed by our fathers appear;
Happenings vast and momentous
  Proclaim that Thy coming is near.

Coming, coming, Jesus my Lord!
  Even so, come, Lord Jesus.[40]

Heart Response

Paul's heart is certainly riveted on the Lord. As his thoughts lead him to long for his Lord's second coming, Paul breaks forth in a roll call of God's attributes! Yes, Paul's vision is elsewhere—not on temporal "things" like money and possessions. In the midst of fighting his own fight for the faith, his focus is upward...godward. These few verses show us where Paul's heart was—it was on godliness, on eternal life, on the fact of God's presence, on Jesus Christ, on His second coming, on the King of kings and Lord of lords, on immortality, on the unapproachable light, on the everlasting!

Where are your sights set, dear sister? As a woman after God's own heart, you, like Paul and like Timothy, are to seek those things which are above and to set your mind on things above, not on things on the earth (Colossians 3:1-2). Let's look upward together!

Lesson 23

Handling Riches

1 Timothy 6:17-19

o you perhaps remember looking briefly at the life of Lot in Lesson 21? Lot was the nephew of God's servant and friend, Abraham. A problem arose between this uncle and nephew because each of them possessed great riches and vast herds of livestock. Unfortunately, Lot's lust and greed led him to make a very poor choice. As the saying goes, "What you do with your money tells what it has done to you."[41] In Lot's case, his decision told on him!

Anyway, the Bible text in Genesis 13:2 describes Abraham in this way: "Abram was very rich." As I studied further, I learned that the Hebrew words here signify that Abraham "was very heavy." Commenting on this term, one commentator-of-old shared this insight into the burden of handling riches wisely.

> *T*here is a burden of care in getting them, fear in keeping them, temptation in using them, guilt in abusing them, sorrow in losing them, and a burden of account, at last, to be given up concerning them.[42]

Today we are allowed to sit in the front row in the apostle Paul's classroom and learn firsthand how to handle riches... *God's* way. Shhhh! The master teacher speaks!

1 Timothy 6:17-19

[17] Command those who are rich in this present age not to be haughty, nor to trust in uncertain riches but in the living God, who gives us richly all things to enjoy.

[18] Let them do good, that they be rich in good works, ready to give, willing to share,

[19] storing up for themselves a good foundation for the time to come, that they may lay hold on eternal life.

Out of God's Word...

In 1 Timothy 6:9 (Lesson 21) Paul dealt with "those who desire to be rich." Now to complete his thoughts on the subject, he deals with "those who *are* rich" (1 Timothy 6:17, emphasis added). Paul is not condemning these believers for their riches. But he is warning them to handle their riches wisely.

1. Against what temptations are the rich warned (verse 17)?

   Who were they to trust in instead (verse 17)?

   How is God described in verse 17?

2. What are the four duties the rich are to be engaged in (verse 18)?

   _____   _____

   _____   _____

3. By sharing their earthly treasures, what greater treasure will the rich receive (verse 19)?

...and into Your Heart

• *Laying up treasure*—What does Jesus say about laying up treasure in Matthew 6:19-21?

   And what does Jesus say about laying up treasure in Luke 12:15-21?

   And what does James have to say about riches (James 5:2)?

Your Checkbook

*H*ave you ever thought of your checkbook as a diary? Like pictures, the checkbook entries speak a thousand words. If a stranger came into possession of your checkbook, what would he or she conclude about your values? About your stewardship? About how you honor God?[43]

Now...take out your checkbook and read your "diary." What tale is told regarding your heart and your values and your way of handling riches? Take note of the checks you've written during the past month. Did your treasure go to the mall...or to ministry? Was your treasure spent for curtains...or for the church? Remember that Paul did not condemn the fact that you have treasure; he just warned about its use and usefulness.

- *Laying hold on eternal life*—Salvation for the rich doesn't come by their giving their wealth away. As with everyone, they must put their faith and trust in Jesus Christ. But the fruit of that salvation is seen in their attitude toward others.

How did Zacchaeus respond to his newfound salvation in Luke 19:8-9?

- *Laying hold of good works*—Giving doesn't require that we have money. Many of the women of the Bible gave out of their poverty. They were truly "rich in good works"! Their hearts of gold shone forth out of the darkness of their poverty. So even if you seem to have little or nothing to give, you can follow in the footsteps of their good works.

What did the widow of Zarephath give to God's prophet Elijah in 1 Kings 17:8-16?

What did Dorcas give to the widows in Acts 9:36-39?

And what did the sisters Mary and Martha give to Jesus and His disciples in Luke 10:38?

What can you share with someone today? A meal? Some needed article of clothing? A deed of kindness? A good word? A smile?

Heart Response

Wasn't that a fun-but-revealing exercise we did regarding our checkbooks?

Well, now let me tell you about a woman who handled her riches in such a way that her checkbook told a glorious tale! C.T. Studd was a wealthy and well-educated Englishman who sailed away to China in 1885 to become one of its first missionaries. Later, before his second trip to China, this man gave away all his wealth except for his last 3,400 British pounds. In his own words, he "invested in the Bank of Heaven."

And the 3,400 pounds? This sum C.T. Studd presented to his wife-to-be as a wedding gift.

However, she asked, "Now, Charlie, what did the Lord tell the rich young man to do?"

When C.T. answered, "Sell all," she said, "Well, then, we will start clear with the Lord at our wedding." She then anonymously gave the 3,400 pounds to General Booth of the Salvation Army.[44]

Dear friend, God may not be asking you to sell all or give away all. But He is asking you and me to prayerfully consider how we are handling our riches. We are *so* blessed! Now let us also bless others!

esson 24

Guarding the Treasure

1 Timothy 6:20-21

I absolutely *love* to sit and listen to my husband preach! Seminary-trained and an ordained pastor and a seminary professor for many years, Jim has much to share from the Word of God!

And perhaps one of my favorite images from one of Jim's messages comes from 2 Timothy 1:14: "Guard, through the Holy Spirit who dwells in us, the treasure which has been entrusted to you" (NASB). To illustrate this truth, Jim launches into a story of our trip to a missions meeting in England. One day during "free time," we visited the famed Tower of London. Inside fortified walls and behind leaded vault doors lay many of the British Empire's crown jewels and articles of gold, protected by armed guards and elaborate alarm systems. All of this—along with video cameras and metal detectors—was necessary to protect and guard the invaluable (and unbelievable to look at!) treasures of England!

But in 2 Timothy 1:14 and in our text here in 1 Timothy 6, Paul tells Timothy that there is an even greater treasure that must be guarded. Let's listen in as Paul gives his final instruction to Timothy about guarding the treasure of the truth of the Word of God.

1 Timothy 6:20-21

20 O Timothy! Guard what was committed to your trust, avoiding the profane and vain babblings and contradictions of what is falsely called knowledge—

21 by professing it, some have strayed concerning the faith. Grace be with you. Amen.

Out of God's Word...

1. First of all, read again and note what was entrusted to *Paul* in 1 Timothy 1:11.

   Now what does Paul ask *Timothy* to guard (1 Timothy 6:20)?

   And what was Timothy to avoid (verse 20)?

2. This may seem like a repeat, but it's important: How does Paul describe what is "falsely called knowledge" (verse 20)?

What devastating effect can false knowledge have on some (verse 21)?

How does Paul end this letter to Timothy (verse 21)?

(And a bonus question: How did Paul begin this letter to Timothy in 1 Timothy 1:2?)

...and into Your Heart

Once again, Paul has positive and negative advice for Timothy, something he is to do...and something he is not to do.

• First the *positive:* What was Timothy to do (verse 20)?

The phrase "to guard" means "to stand as a watchman." In other words, Timothy was to stand as a soldier guarding a treasure which had been entrusted to him for safe-keeping.

And the phrase "what was committed to your trust" translates one Greek word which means "deposit." The deposit or "treasure" Timothy was to guard was the truth—the divine revelation, the true gospel, the sound doctrine of "the glorious gospel of the blessed God" (1 Timothy 1:11).

What are some ways to guard the priceless truths that have been entrusted to you?

• Now for the *negative:* What was Timothy not to participate in (verse 20)?

Also, in chapter 1 of 1 Timothy, "some" had strayed from the truth by doing what?

1 Timothy 1:4—They gave heed to _____ and _____.

1 Timothy 1:6—They turned aside to _____.

It's so easy to get caught up in profane and idle babblings, in fables, and in idle talk. Use the following lists for personal evaluation:

Your associations—Who is giving the most input into your life? And are they feeding you with "wholesome" and "healthy" words (1 Timothy 6:3), or are they filling your mind with profane, vain babblings, and idle talk? (I can't help it, but TV talk shows come quickly to mind!)

Your reading material—Are you reading "wholesome" and "healthy" material, or are you feeding on the profane (irrelevant), and on fables (novels of questionable content)? Are you perhaps reading too much fiction (fables)?

Your conversations—Are your talks with both believers and unbelievers focused on God and His Word, or are they centered on the world and worldliness (vain babbling)?

Your studies—Are your studies centered on the pure milk and meat of the Word, or are you studying too much "falsely called knowledge" that contradicts Scripture?

Now, what must you do to pursue the positive (the truth) and avoid the negative (false knowledge)?

Heart Response

Dear Paul! He's finally finished. And so this powerful mentor simply closes his passionate and instructive letter to his young friend and son in the faith with these four priceless and packed words:

~Grace be with you~

Perhaps when this has been said, all has been said! Why? Because grace is God's unmerited favor. Paul had opened this letter with God's grace (1 Timothy 1:2). And now he closes it with God's grace. For Paul, God's grace was never just a trite social greeting, but it was a costly gift from God. Having so often experienced the grace of God, Paul never ceased to pray that others would experience that same grace.

Are you drawing upon the rich resource of God's grace, dear one? Timothy needed it. And you do, too. May you treasure God's grace and favor as you continue pursuing a life of godliness!

Lesson 25

A Final Word

Summary of 1 Timothy

"Godliness" is a word we, as Christians, love to throw around. We emote over it, pray for it, and speak of it often. But hopefully, after 24 lessons on what it means to pursue godliness, you have a better understanding of it. Godliness, as we've learned, is desiring to please God by walking in His ways. It is "God-ward-ness." And the woman who pursues godliness has her focus on God and on following His commands.

I mentioned earlier in our study that the word "godliness" is used eight times in this letter from Paul to Timothy. As a final exercise, please read these references again. Write out the Scriptures, if you wish. But be sure and note the issue or the behavior that has to do with godliness.

1 Timothy 2:2—

1 Timothy 2:10—

1 Timothy 3:16—

1 Timothy 4:7-8—

1 Timothy 6:3—

1 Timothy 6:5—

1 Timothy 6:6—

1 Timothy 6:11—

And now, before we close, I want to share an acrostic of the book of 1 Timothy, which spells out the word **A-D-V-I-C-E**. Under each chapter, write down some of the advice given.

Chapter 1   **A** dvice concerning false teachings

Chapter 2   **D** irections for godly women

Chapter 3   **V** irtues of Christian elders

Chapter 4   **I** nstruction for godly living

Chapter 5   **C** ounsel concerning the widows

Chapter 6   **E** ffects of worldly living[45]

Paul was a godly man who pursued godliness. His focus was on God and following His commands. God-ward-ness was a lifestyle for Paul. As an outpouring of his heart, Paul began this letter with a doxology (1:17) and ended it with another (6:15-16). Read both doxologies now and spend some time thanking God for His many wonderful attributes, and make a fresh commitment to Him to further pursue godliness as your lifestyle. May our dear Lord bless you as you continue in such a God-ward pursuit. "Grace be with you," my dear friend.

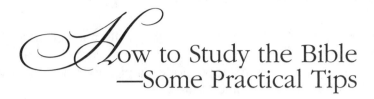

How to Study the Bible
—Some Practical Tips

By Jim George, Th.M.

One of the noblest pursuits a child of God can embark upon is to get to know and understand God better. The best way we can accomplish this is to look carefully at the book He has written, the Bible, which communicates who He is and His plan for mankind. There are a number of ways we can study the Bible, but one of the most effective and simple approaches to reading and understanding God's Word involves three simple steps:

Step 1: Observation—*What does the passage say?*

Step 2: Interpretation—*What does the passage mean?*

Step 3: Application—*What am I going to do about what the passage says and means?*

Observation is the first and most important step in the process. As you read the Bible text, you need to *look* carefully at what is said, and how. Look for:

- *Terms, not words.* Words can have many meanings, but terms are words used in a specific way in a specific context. (For instance, the word *trunk* could apply to a tree, a car, or a storage box. However, when you read, "That tree has a very large trunk," you know exactly what the word means, which makes it a term.)

- *Structure.* If you look at your Bible, you will see that the text has units called *paragraphs* (indented or marked ¶). A paragraph is a complete unit of thought. You can discover the content of the author's message by noting and understanding each paragraph unit.

- *Emphasis.* The amount of space or the number of chapters or verses devoted to a specific topic will reveal the importance of that topic (for example, note the emphasis of Romans 9–11 and Psalm 119).

- *Repetition.* This is another way an author demonstrates that something is important. One reading of 1 Corinthians 13, where the author uses the word "love" nine times in only 13 verses, communicates to us that love is the focal point of these 13 verses.

- *Relationships between ideas.* Pay close attention, for example, to certain relationships that appear in the text:

  —Cause-and-effect: "Well done, good and faithful servant; you were faithful over a few things, I will make you ruler over many things" (Matthew 25:21).

  —Ifs and thens: "If My people who are called by My name will humble themselves, and pray and seek My face, and turn from their wicked ways, then I will hear from heaven and forgive their sin and heal their land" (2 Chronicles 7:14).

  —Questions and answers: "Who is the King of glory? The Lord strong and mighty" (Psalm 24:8).

- *Comparisons and contrasts.* For example, "You have heard that it was said...but I say to you..." (Matthew 5:21).

- *Literary form.* The Bible is literature, and the three main types of literature in the Bible are discourse (the epistles), prose (Old Testament history), and poetry (the Psalms). Considering the type of literature makes a great deal of difference when you read and interpret the Scriptures.

- *Atmosphere.* The author had a particular reason or burden for writing each passage, chapter, and book. Be sure you notice the mood or tone or urgency of the writing.

After you have considered these things, you then are ready to ask the "Wh" questions:

Who?   Who are the people in this passage?
What?   What is happening in this passage?
Where?   Where is this story taking place?
When?   What time (of day, of the year, in history) is it?

Asking these four "Wh" questions can help you notice terms and identify atmosphere. The answers will also enable you to use your imagination to re-create the scene you're reading about.

As you answer the "Wh" questions and imagine the event, you'll probably come up with some questions of your own. Asking those additional questions for understanding will help to build a bridge between observation (the first step) and interpretation (the second step) of the Bible study process.

Interpretation is discovering the meaning of a passage, the author's main thought or idea. Answering the questions that arise during observation will help you in the process of interpretation. Five clues (called "the five C's") can help you determine the author's main point(s):

• *Context.* You can answer 75 percent of your questions about a passage when you read the text. Reading the text involves looking at the near context (the verse immediately before and after) as well as the far context (the paragraph or the chapter that precedes and/or follows the passage you're studying).

• *Cross-references.* Let Scripture interpret Scripture. That is, let other passages in the Bible shed light on the passage you are looking at. At the same time, be careful not to assume that the same word or phrase in two different passages means the same thing.

- *Culture*. The Bible was written long ago, so when we interpret it, we need to understand it from the writers' cultural context.

- *Conclusion*. Having answered your questions for understanding by means of context, cross-reference, and culture, you can make a preliminary statement of the passage's meaning. Remember that if your passage consists of more than one paragraph, the author may be presenting more than one thought or idea.

- *Consultation*. Reading books known as commentaries, which are written by Bible scholars, can help you interpret Scripture.

Application is why we study the Bible. We want our lives to change; we want to be obedient to God and to grow more like Jesus Christ. After we have observed a passage and interpreted or understood it to the best of our ability, we must then apply its truth to our own life.

You'll want to ask the following questions of every passage of Scripture you study:

- How does the truth revealed here affect my relationship with God?

- How does this truth affect my relationship with others?

- How does this truth affect me?

- How does this truth affect my response to the enemy Satan?

The application step is not completed by simply answering these questions; the key is *putting into practice* what God has taught you in your study. Although at any given moment you cannot be consciously applying *every*-thing you're learning in Bible study, you can be consciously applying *some*thing. And when you work on applying a truth to your life, God will bless your efforts by, as noted earlier, conforming you to the image of Jesus Christ.

Helpful Bible Study Resources

Concordance—Young's or Strong's

Bible dictionary—Unger's or Holman's

Webster's dictionary

The Zondervan Pictorial Encyclopedia of the Bible

Manners and Customs of the Bible, James M. Freeman

Books on Bible Study

The Joy of Discovery, Oletta Wald

Enjoy Your Bible, Irving L. Jensen

How to Read the Bible for All It's Worth, Gordon Fee & Douglas Stuart

A Layman's Guide to Interpreting the Bible, W. Henrichsen

Living by the Book, Howard G. Hendricks

Notes

1. Taken from Elizabeth George, *A Woman After God's Own Heart*™ (Eugene, OR: Harvest House Publishers, 1997), pp. 24-29.
2. William Hendricksen, *New Testament Commentary—Exposition of the Pastoral Epistles* (Grand Rapids, MI: Baker Book House, 1976), p. 49.
3. D. Edmond Hiebert, *Everyman's Bible Commentary—First Timothy* (Chicago: Moody Press, 1957), p. 22.
4. D. L. Moody, *Notes from My Bible and Quotes from My Library*—quoting Charles H. Spurgeon (Grand Rapids, MI: Baker Book House, 1979), p. 329.
5. Ben Patterson, *Waiting—Finding Hope When God Seems Silent* (Downers Grove, IL: InterVarsity Press, 1989), p. 153.
6. Hiebert, *Everyman's Bible Commentary,* quoting J. P. Lilley, p. 44.
7. Bruce B. Barton, David R. Veerman, and Neil Wilson, *Life Application Bible Commentary—1 & 2 Timothy & Titus* (Wheaton, IL: Tyndale House Publishers, Inc., 1993), p. 35.
8. Hendricksen, *New Testament Commentary,* p. 86.
9. Barton, Veerman, and Wilson, *Life Application Bible Commentary,* p. 36.
10. Hiebert, *Everyman's Bible Commentary,* p. 50.
11. *John MacArthur's Bible Studies,* "Church Leadership," *1 Timothy 3:1-13* (Panorama City, CA: Grace to You, 1989), p. 16.
12. Karen Burton Mains, *Open Heart, Open Home* (Elgin, IL: David C. Cook, 1976).
13. Elizabeth George, *Beautiful in God's Eyes—The Treasures of the Proverbs 31 Woman,* citing John MacArthur, "God's High Calling for Women," Part 4, Panorama City, CA: Word of Grace, #GC-54-17, 1986 (Eugene, OR: Harvest House Publishers, 1998), p. 161.
14. Hiebert, *Everyman's Bible Commentary,* p. 71.
15. Elizabeth George, *Women Who Loved God—365 Days with the Women of the Bible* (Eugene, OR: Harvest House Publishers, 1999), December 6–9.
16. Robert Jamieson, A. R. Fausset, and David Brown, *Commentary on the Whole Bible* (Grand Rapids, MI: Zondervan Publishing House, 1973), p. 1361.
17. Hendricksen, *New Testament Commentary,* p. 139.
18. Ibid., p. 141.

19. John MacArthur, Jr., *The MacArthur New Testament Commentary—1 Timothy* (Chicago: Moody Press, 1995), p. 143.

20. William T. Summers, ed., *3000 Quotations from the Writings of Matthew Henry* (Grand Rapids, MI: Fleming H. Revell, 1982), p. 310.

21. Ibid.

22. Barton, Veerman, and Wilson, *Life Application Bible Commentary,* p. 80.

23. Hiebert, *Everyman's Bible Commentary,* p. 82.

24. MacArthur, Jr., *The MacArthur New Testament Commentary,* p. 168.

25. Homer Kent, *The Pastoral Epistles* (Chicago: Moody Press, 1977), p. 173.

26. Charles R. Swindoll, *The Tale of the Tardy Oxcart,* quoting John Greenleaf Whittier (Nashville, TN: Word Publishing Inc., 1998), pp. 230-31.

27. Hiebert, *Everyman's Bible Commentary,* p. 98.

28. MacArthur, Jr., *The MacArthur New Testament Commentary,* pp. 213-14.

29. Drawn from George, *Women Who Loved God—365 Days with the Women of the Bible,* December 11.

30. Barton, Veerman, and Wilson, *Life Application Bible Commentary,* p. 108.

31. Eleanor L. Doan, *The Speaker's Sourcebook,* author unknown (Grand Rapids, MI: Zondervan Publishing House, 1977), p. 116.

32. MacArthur, Jr., *The MacArthur New Testament Commentary,* p. 240.

33. Jamieson, Fausset, and Brown, *Commentary on the Whole Bible,* p. 1369.

34. Ibid.

35. Charles F. Pfeiffer and Everett F. Harrison, *The Wycliffe Bible Commentary* (Chicago: Moody Press, 1973), p. 1379.

36. Summers, ed., *3000 Quotations,* p. 310.

37. Hiebert, *Everyman's Bible Commentary,* p. 118.

38. Ibid., p. 116.

39. Ibid.

40. J. Sidlow Baxter, *Explore the Book* (Grand Rapids, MI: Zondervan Publishing House, 173), p. 242.

41. M. R. DeHaan and Henry G. Bosch, *Our Daily Bread* (Grand Rapids, MI: Zondervan Publishing House, 1982), April 2.

42. Matthew Henry, *Commentary on the Whole Bible—Volume 1* (Peabody, MA: Hendrickson Publishers, 1996), p. 72.

43. Barton, Veerman, and Wilson, *Life Application Bible Commentary,* p. 127.

44. Norman Grubb, *C. T. Studd* (Grand Rapids, MI: Zondervan Publishing House, 1946), pp. 50-69.

45. Barry Huddleston, *The Acrostic Bible* (Portland, OR: Walk Thru the Bible Press, Inc., 1978).

Bibliography

Barton, Bruce, B., David R. Veerman, and Neil Wilson. *Life Application Bible Commentary—1 Timothy, 2 Timothy, and Titus*. Wheaton, IL: Tyndale House Publishers, Inc., 1993.

Guthrie, Donald. *Tyndale New Testament Commentaries—The Pastoral Epistles*. Grand Rapids, MI: Wm. B. Eerdmans Publishing Company, 1976.

Hendricksen, William. *New Testament Commentary—Exposition of the Pastoral Epistles*. Grand Rapids, MI: Baker Book House, 1976.

Hiebert, D. Edmond. *Everyman's Bible Commentary—First Timothy*. Chicago: Moody Press, 1957.

Jamieson, Robert, A. R. Fausset, and David Brown. *Commentary on the Whole Bible*. Grand Rapids, MI: Zondervan Publishing House, 1973.

Kent, Homer. *The Pastoral Epistles*. Chicago: Moody Press, 1977.

MacArthur, Jr., John. *The MacArthur New Testament Commentary—1 Timothy*. Chicago: Moody Press, 1995.

Pfeiffer, Charles F. and Everett F. Harrison. *The Wycliffe Bible Commentary*. Chicago: Moody Press, 1973.

About the Author

Elizabeth George is a bestselling author and speaker whose passion is to teach the Bible in a way that changes women's lives. For information about Elizabeth's books or speaking ministry, to sign up for her mailings, or to share how God has used this book in your life, please write to Elizabeth at:

Elizabeth George
P.O. Box 2879
Belfair, WA 98528

Toll-free fax/phone: 1-800-542-4611
www.elizabethgeorge.com

~

A Woman After God's Own Heart® Study Series

BIBLE STUDIES FOR BUSY WOMEN

"God wrote the Bible to change hearts and lives. Every study in this series is written with that in mind—and is specially focused on helping Christian women know how God desires for them to live."

—Elizabeth George

Sharing wisdom gleaned from more than 20 years as a women's Bible study teacher, Elizabeth has prepared insightful lessons that can be completed in 15 to 20 minutes per day. Each lesson includes thought-provoking questions and insights, Bible study tips, instructions for leading a discussion group, and a "heart response" section to make the Bible passage more personal.

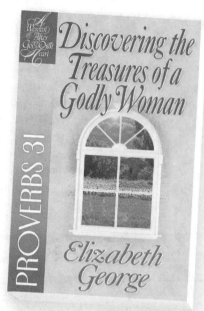

Proverbs 31 0-7369-0818-8

Philippians 0-7369-0289-9

1 Peter 0-7369-0290-2

1 Timothy 0-7369-0665-7

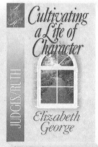

Judges/Ruth 0-7369-0498-0

Esther 0-7369-0489-1

James 0-7369-0490-5

Life of Mary 0-7369-0300-3

Life of Sarah 0-7369-0301-1

Books by Elizabeth George

Beautiful in God's Eyes—The Treasures of the Proverbs 31 Woman
Powerful Promises for Every Woman
Life Management for Busy Women
Loving God with All Your Mind
A Woman After God's Own Heart®
A Woman After God's Own Heart® Deluxe Edition
A Woman After God's Own Heart® Audiobook
A Woman After God's Own Heart® Prayer Journal
A Woman's High Calling—10 Essentials for Godly Living
A Woman's Walk with God—Growing in the Fruit of the Spirit
Women Who Loved God—365 Days with the Women of the Bible
A Young Woman After God's Own Heart

Growth & Study Guides

Powerful Promises for Every Woman Growth & Study Guide
Life Management for Busy Women Growth & Study Guide
A Woman After God's Own Heart® Growth & Study Guide
A Woman's High Calling Growth & Study Guide
A Woman's Walk with God Growth & Study Guide

A Woman After God's Own Heart® Bible Study Series

Walking in God's Promises—The Life of Sarah
Cultivating a Life of Character—Judges/Ruth
Becoming a Woman of Beauty & Strength—Esther
Discovering the Treasures of a Godly Woman—Proverbs 31
Nurturing a Heart of Humility—The Life of Mary
Experiencing God's Peace—Philippians
Pursuing Godliness—1 Timothy
Growing in Wisdom & Faith—James
Putting On a Gentle & Quiet Spirit—1 Peter

Children's Books

God's Wisdom for Little Boys—Character-Building Fun from Proverbs
(co-authored with Jim George)
God's Wisdom for Little Girls—Virtues & Fun from Proverbs 31
God's Little Girl Is Helpful
God's Little Girl Is Kind